MUSIC with BABIES and YOUNG CHILDREN

Activities to Encourage Bonding, Communication and Wellbeing

Jeffrey Friedberg

Illustrations by Chlöe Applin

Jessica Kingsley Publishers
London and Philadelphia

First published in 2020
by Jessica Kingsley Publishers
73 Collier Street
London N1 9BE, UK
and
400 Market Street, Suite 400
Philadelphia, PA 19106, USA

www.jkp.com

Copyright © Jeffrey Friedberg 2020
Illustrations copyright © Chlöe Applin 2020

Front cover image source: Chlöe Applin.

Library of Congress Cataloging in Publication Data
A CIP catalog record for this book is available from the Library of Congress

British Library Cataloguing in Publication Data
A CIP catalogue record for this book is available from the British Library

ISBN 978 1 78592 764 5
eISBN 978 1 78450 635 3

Printed and bound in the United States

The accompanying music and video files for select songs can be downloaded
from www.jkp.com/voucher using the code BOOMESE.

This book is dedicated to all parents who are willing to celebrate the joys and embrace the challenges of parenting—through music—and to the children who show us the true purpose of music.

Contents

Disclaimer 8

Acknowledgments 9

Introduction 10

1. Music Matters 17

2. Bonding through Music 35

3. Friends through Music 51

4. Sleep through Music 90

5. Physical Fitness and Motor Development through Music . . . 111

6. Learning, Language, Literacy, Math Skills and School
   Readiness through Music 150

7. Managing Feelings and Developing Focus through Music . . 185

8. Diversity through Music 214

Conclusion 236

References 238

Disclaimer

The information contained in this book is not intended to replace the services of trained medical professionals or to be a substitute for medical advice. You are advised to consult a doctor on any matters relating to your health or your child's health, and in particular on any matters that may require diagnosis or medical attention.

Every effort has been made to trace copyright holders and to obtain their permission for the use of copyright material (including music) where necessary to do so. The author and the publisher apologize for any omissions and would be grateful if notified of any acknowledgments that should be incorporated in future reprints or editions of this book.

The accompanying music and video files for select songs can be downloaded from www.jkp.com/voucher using the code BOOMESE.

Acknowledgments

Thank you to my wife Beth for your support and help in writing this book! I couldn't have done it without you. Your parenting skills are an inspiration.

Thank you to my wonderful children, Zoe and Eva, for being amazing kids and for helping me be a better parent and person.

Thank you to Jessica Kingsley Publishers and your great team for believing in and supporting me in publishing this book!

Thank you to Ginny Blanford for your awesome guidance in editing my manuscript. You really helped me pull it all together.

Thank you to Jed Baker for helping review parts of the book and giving me your thoughtful feedback. Always appreciated!

Thank you to my music therapy intern, Rachel Lessick, for all of your early help in gathering research and articles for the book!

Finally, thank you to all the children and parents who have allowed me to help you access your inner musicians. Life is truly a journey and music is truly a process. Thank you for sharing the journey and the process together!

INTRODUCTION

To music is to be human

Music is something we do. Musicologist Christopher Small (1998) coined the word "musicking" to describe the power and meaning of music. For Small, the musical work itself is just one part of the process of music. He sees music not as a noun, but as a verb—a process, not a product. That's what this book is all about.

Musical parenting

Parenting is both a joy and a challenge.

Children bring us incredible joy. Their wide smiles, deep belly laughs and raised arms when they see us are heartwarming. Their eagerness and determination to master new skills is inspiring. Their unconditional love and complete trust in us to keep them safe and help them learn and grow is motivating.

But parenting is also a challenge. Why won't they go to sleep more easily? How can we help them manage difficult feelings? How can we keep them engaged and help them build their attention span and focus? How can we help them make friends and play nicely? How can we encourage kindness and thoughtfulness? What can we do to help them manage transitions better and go to daycare or preschool with less fuss? How can we help them try new things and be less anxious?

And just when you think you've got the hang of a challenge, your child changes, and you feel like you're starting all over again.

I've got two words for you, *musical parenting*. Music can help bring joy to many of the challenges of growing up.

Please note that I use the term "parenting" broadly. It is my sense, and hopefully yours after you read this book, that whether or not you are raising your own or teaching, caregiving or providing therapy to a baby or young child, you are essentially "parenting". In many ways you are a surrogate parent in that you are bonding with a child in helping them feel safe and secure and feeling that their needs will be met relatively quickly and consistently. You are also, hopefully, guiding them in having the experiences and learning the skills they need to develop and reach their potential as best they can. I also use the term "your child" throughout the book to refer to one's own children as well as one's student, client or patient. Please keep this in mind as you read through this book.

Why is music important in the early years?

The early years are incredibly important for a child's development. Young children's brains are developing at an unprecedented rate. They are building skills that are the foundation for all future development. Research continues to tell us more and more every day about the huge impact that the early years have on how we function as adults.

More specifically, research shows that music can help children develop skills and confidence in all areas—and even develop bigger and faster brains! (More about this in Chapter 1.) Musical parenting is essentially tapping into our brain's natural musical abilities. We are pre-wired to make music—our brains have evolved to use music for survival, for communication, for the passing down of knowledge. Humans have used music in parenting for ages (possibly before we even developed language), to help children learn, grow and develop. Building a relationship with your child through music can be incredibly meaningful, intimate and educational.

While music can be beautiful to hear and skilled performers amazing to watch, music's ultimate benefits are more than aesthetic. The power of music is in how it helps us throughout our lives to manage the challenges, and experience the joys, of being human. The power of parenting through music lies in the process, rather than the product, of using music to help us survive; music is simply something we do.

Music can help you parent better and more confidently. When we parent intentionally, purposefully and constructively with music, we are helping our children develop optimally in order to be their best selves.

Why did I write this book?

As a new parent, over 20 years ago, I was resistant to the parenting method books that my wife thoughtfully tried to get me to read.

With my kids I wanted an organic and intuitive process to guide our relationships and their development. I didn't want to stick my nose in a book or take anyone else's advice. Looking back, I realize this was more than a little contradictory. As a board-certified music therapist, I was using a wide range of books and theories to guide my music therapy work with children and adults with a variety of challenges and needs. But this felt different.

I didn't want to consult any parenting books with my own children. I wanted to be more "in the moment" with them, making forts out of cardboard boxes, reading the classic children's books, and singing and drumming together. I wanted to draw from my own experiences growing up to guide my parenting. I thought I knew all the ways to help my kids have the best childhood possible.

But as they grew, I realized I needed help with the challenging moments. This parenting thing wasn't quite as easy as I had imagined. I came to embrace having a balance between being in the moment with my children, spending some time learning and understanding how they develop, and creating a "tool kit" of strategies to use in the challenging moments. A little knowledge went a long way in helping me be a better parent and in helping my children manage the process of growing up. So now that my children are more or less grown, it seems like the right time to share what I've learned about music and children—from both being a parent and from my 24 years as a music therapist—with other parents and caregivers.

My goal in writing *Music with Babies and Young Children* has been to combine knowledge, theory and science with musical activities and experiences. I want *Music with Babies and Young Children* both to help you be more "in the moment" with your children, enabling them to have playful and organic experiences that improve their development, and to provide some fun, easy-to-use and evidence-based activities and strategies.

I have tried to organize what we know about child development and music into a creative and practical approach to parenting and raising young children. I have tried to show how we are a musical species, and the reason we have music is not simply aesthetic, but perhaps more importantly for enhancing health and wellbeing, learning and development.

I have tried to make music accessible to everyone, musicians and non-musicians alike, to use on a daily basis in order to be more effective, confident and creative in their parenting. Ultimately, I hope this book, and approach, helps children to have happier childhoods through accessing their "inner musicians."

Who is *Music with Babies and Young Children* for?

Music with Babies and Young Children is for anyone who has meaningful contact with young children, aged 0–5 years old. *Music with Babies and Young Children* is for parents as well as grandparents, teachers, childcare providers, physicians and therapists. *Music with Babies and Young Children* is for people who parent or work with children who are developing typically or atypically, or who have suffered injury or trauma. *Music with Babies and Young Children* is for people who want to help children learn, grow and develop in a way that is in tune with their brains, minds and bodies.

No musical skills necessary!

Don't worry, you don't have to have any musical skills or training to "musically parent." No experience is necessary to sing, dance or tap a tambourine in order to help a child flourish. You just need a willingness, enthusiasm and openness to tap into your brain's inner musician. Music is for everyone.

We are all born musicians

But maybe you've lost touch with your "inner musician." We all have musical brains that just need a little encouragement and guidance. My recommendation is to put aside your judgments and pride, engage in heartfelt, enthusiastic music-making and see what happens.

Obviously, it's more fun if you can keep a beat and sing in tune, but the more you try the better you'll get! You just have to wake up your musical brain and start singing and dancing. And your children will love the time spent making music together. They'll most likely care more about your eagerness, earnestness and openness than your musical skills. To them you'll always be a rock star!

It doesn't hurt, however, if you want to take a guitar or ukulele lesson along the way. Learning new music skills is fun, will help your brain and body as you age, and will help you show your children that musical expression (and learning new things) is for everyone.

Why should you listen to me?

Let's start with the official credentials: In addition to my being a parent of two wonderful young adult children, I am also a board-certified music therapist for almost 25 years, a New York State licensed creative arts therapist, and a children's musician for over 20 years. I have an MA in music therapy from New York University. I currently run Music for Life Creative Arts Therapy PLLC in Nyack, New York.

As a music therapist, I use music on a daily basis to help people build physical, social-emotional, cognitive, and language and communication skills. I use music to help people engage in meaningful expression and communication and build healing relationships. I use music to help people developing typically and atypically, including people with developmental delays and disabilities, autism, ADHD, social and behavioral challenges, traumatic brain injury, Alzheimer's and dementia, and people managing difficult life transitions of deaths and separations in their families.

As a children's musician, I created and have led The Bossy Frog Band for over 20 years. I have recorded eight albums of music for children and performed for over 130,000 children and families. I sing and play banjo, guitar, harmonica and saxophone. I also play banjo in a "not-to-be-missed-if-you're-in-NYC-on-a-Monday-night" bluegrass band, The Crusty Gentlemen.

But here's the more important credential: Music saved my life

I was always drawn to music on a primitive, emotional level. Music spoke to me deeply. I remember my mother taking me to early childhood music classes when I was five years old; going to these classes was a special time for me to share with her. I was a shy child, and the musical activities were freeing. They offered me an opportunity to be more expressive and creative than I usually was. A few years later, in elementary school, one of my most vivid memories is of our music teacher, Ms. Forster, coming into our fourth-grade classroom to demonstrate the instruments that we would be able to take lessons on the following year. When she leaned back, closed her eyes and blew riffs on the shiny alto saxophone, I was transported to another universe. I can still see and feel the fireworks going off in me when she played. I ended up studying the saxophone all the way through high school and eventually performed professionally for several years!

In my sophomore year of high school, my mother was diagnosed with ovarian cancer. I wasn't a very verbally expressive adolescent; I had limited tools and resources to deal with the deeply painful feelings both of helping her fight this horrible disease and of watching her slowly fade away. As her illness worsened, I immersed myself in music, intensely studying jazz saxophone. I had lost confidence in the stability of the world, and music became my salvation—a life raft that offered a way to express my pain without using words. My music also brought me intimate friendships, deep and special, that helped me survive those very difficult years.

When my mother passed away two years after her diagnosis, music continued to support me. In life I was adrift, but music centered my world. Playing, listening and writing music, along with the relationships I formed through music, helped me navigate this difficult time. Eventually, I realized that I wanted to understand this healing power of music. That's when I chose music therapy as my career.

For the last 24 years, I have been exploring, experimenting with and learning how music can help others learn, grow and develop. I am thankful for music and the many deep relationships it has helped me form and the skills and understanding it has helped me to build in myself and others.

How to use *Music with Babies and Young Children*

Music with Babies and Young Children begins with two "big picture" chapters: Music Matters, and Bonding through Music. These will give you a good background, and I'd suggest that you read them first, and then jump around through the other chapters based on your specific interests or challenges at any particular moment.

Chapter organization

Chapters 2–8 of *Music with Babies and Young Children* are organized consistently. Each one begins with a section on child development theory in the chapter's area of focus, followed by a section on how music can help with that specific area of development. The final section of each chapter is the "meat and potatoes": songs, games and activities that you can immediately apply. Chapters focus on a wide variety of areas where music can be useful: creating bonds; developing a healthy sense of self; managing thoughts, feelings and bodies independently;

developing social skills and making friends; helping build healthy sleep hygiene; building physical skills and fitness; learning how to learn and increase communication and language skills; and exploring—and appreciating—cultural differences. When we use music every day in the simple moments, we can help our children learn to manage many of the challenges, and increase the joys, of growing up. We'll learn, surprisingly, that many songs we grew up with and thought were simple games or party songs—"If You're Happy and You Know It" and "Ring Around the Rosie," for example—are much more than they seem: in fact, they are brain-, mind-, body-, relationship- and culture-expanding party songs. Music is quite amazing…and useful.

Songs, games and activities

The activities in this book include lyrics, but you will also want music for many of these. The accompanying music and video files can be downloaded from www.jkp.com/voucher using the code BOOMESE. Please feel free to use these to learn the songs. I do encourage you, however, to try to sing the songs with and to your child, and have them sing them for you, rather than just play the recordings for your children. Or at least try to sing along with the recordings!

You will find some of the songs, games and activities more useful and enjoyable than others. Please explore, experiment and find which work best for you, your individual child and your unique family, session room or classroom.

Each song, game and activity is followed by a section where you can write "notes." I encourage you to keep track of which music works well for your child and family and how you, your child and family adapt each for your particular interests and needs. You'll have fun looking back on these notes as your children grow!

I hope you have fun as you go forth and musically parent!

1

MUSIC MATTERS

Musical Experiences Matter in the Development of Brains, Minds, Bodies, Relationships, Families and Communities

The musicologist Christopher Small (1998) writes that music is more than just the actual "sound creation." "Musicking," to use his term, is a way of relating, expressing, communicating, learning and being in relationship. All aspects of music, from the composer to the performers to the audience to the ticket-takers to the people who clean up after the show to the people who design concert halls (and the design of the halls themselves) to the identities formed around music and musicians to the structure of the performances, and more, are important. They all have meaning.

The product vs. process of music

The *product* of music, the song or recording or pop star or specific performance, has limited power on its own. The primary focus on this aspect of music is really just a creation of mass-media. It's part of the music business. There's nothing wrong with that. I've been in the music business for years and benefit when people buy my "music." I love sharing my music as a product. It makes me feel good when people enjoy and purchase my musical creations and it helps me support my family.

But the product of music can often be more like the extra salt they put on potato chips: It's not always about learning and growth. The goal of the "salt" is often to trick our brains into wanting more potato chips. It's not necessarily nutrition.

The nutrition, or power, of music lies in the *process* of music. The important aspects of the process of music for young children include:

17

the relationships formed, the multi-sensory stimulation experienced, the cause-and-effect relationships figured out, the information and skills learned and the personal and cultural identity built. All aspects of music contribute to its power—melody, rhythm, harmony, timbre (the specific sound), dynamics (volume), tempo (speed) and articulation (how each note is played), as well as how we engage in music, including: singing, playing instruments, dancing and moving to music, listening, composing, hearing live music, the actual musical instruments we use and hear, the identities we form around the shared music and musicians we like and know, and more.

Across our entire lifespan, from before birth to the end of life, music functions in different ways at different times to help us grow—and cope. Take a minute to think about the importance of music for infants, in helping form bonds with their parents and caregivers through singing and rocking; for toddlers, in learning language through singing simple songs; for preschoolers, in learning social skills through moving together when singing play songs; or for adolescents, in helping them form their individual and group identities and providing a way of bonding with and organizing their "tribe" of friends. Think about how dancing and love songs help us court our life partners during our early adult years and help maintain our love as we raise our children. Think about how music is part of most religious rituals, helping us manage our existential anxiety and calm our nerves as we get older, or how national anthems are sung to help reinforce our identities as citizens of our country. In *The World in Six Songs*, neuroscientist Daniel Levitin (2016) goes into great detail about how humans have used, and continue to use, music to help us survive in each of these areas.

So, why do we humans "musick," in Small's word? Why is the process of music so important to us?

We have musical brains

Evidence strongly points to the conclusion that humans have evolved "musical brains." It's baked into the cake. We are musical creatures. Human brains evolved to use music to survive, or, as Levitin (2016) writes, "music paved the way for more complex behaviors" (p.3).

Our brains are primed to be receptive to, and to use, music to learn, grow and master skills necessary for survival and abilities for healthy development. Music is not just something that we figured out and passed down to each successive generation (although we do pass down specific styles of music and songs). No—our brains are driven to "musick" because they're "hard-wired" for music, just as they're hard-wired for language.

RESEARCH SHOWS

Author and professor Natalie Sarrazin (2016), in *Music and the Child*, concludes that music satisfies four important criteria that help determine if something is "hard-wired" into the brain: 1) whether or not it is present in all cultures; 2) if the ability to process music appears early in life, i.e. it is found in infants; 3) if examples of music are found in the animal world; and 4) if there are specialized areas of the brain dedicated to it. Music fulfills all of these criteria, and is definitely hard-wired in the human brain.

Music is everywhere. Every culture uses music in some form. Most of us probably don't even realize how ubiquitous music is in our everyday lives. In the USA, on average, Edison Research (2014) found that adults experience over four hours of audio every day, a majority of that being music—and we spend some 13 years of our lives hearing music! Take a minute to think of all the times that you experienced some aspect of music today—from a TV show or video on social media or at a doctor's office, or listening to your headphones while walking, or listening in your car or at the gym, mall or grocery store or while helping your child go to sleep.

Humans have been "musicking" for a long time. Some of the earliest known musical instruments are bone flutes dating back over 40,000 years found in caves in Slovenia and Germany (*The New York Times* 2012). It is highly likely that music-making existed before this with some form of vocalizing, body percussion and stick banging. In his book *The Singing Neanderthals* (2005), Steven Mithen argues that music preceded language as a form of communication in early humans. Now he's not suggesting that our Neanderthal ancestors sat around the campfire singing three-part harmony. But he does lay out a powerful case for a musical form of expression and communication having existed before language as we know it, and that today's music, and language, is related to this early form of expression and communication.

In *The World in Six Songs*, Levitin (2016) theorizes that our musical brains have influenced human development and our ability to live in large civilizations. He suggests that the ability of musically inclined people to understand, express and communicate through music, especially on a feeling level, may have helped our ancestors manage intra- and inter-tribal conflict. In addition to conflict resolution and managing the lifespan events mentioned earlier that are influenced by music, Levitin argues that music also helps in learning skills and storing and transferring data.

And humans engage in music because it feels good in all the right places. Researchers Zatorre and Salimpoor (2013) have found that music, food and sex all stimulate the same pleasure center in our brains. Music must be pretty important for evolution to have put it in this company in our brains!

In order to more deeply understand how musical experiences matter in the early years, let's first explore what and how overall experiences matter in brain, mind, body and cultural development.

Experiences matter

Experiences have a tremendous influence on how young children's brains, minds and bodies develop. Children need our help to provide them with enough quality experiences in order to become their best selves. It is hard to overestimate how important everyday experiences can be in a child's development.

Simply speaking, quality experiences include: safe, loving and trusting relationships in which a child's needs are met responsively; rich multi-sensory stimulation; and engaging opportunities to play and physically explore their environment as they learn how things work. Experiences don't have to be elaborate or expensive. The simplest everyday experiences can provide meaningful opportunities and interactions for learning and growth.

Experiences help shape the architecture of a child's brain. In the early years, our brains form an incredible array of neural connections and networks. These connections enable our young minds to develop a sense of ourselves as unique individuals, with the ability to learn new things, to regulate needs and manage stress, to create the blueprints for forming future relationships, and to assemble the building blocks of our cultural identity. According to many researchers, the early years are the busiest and most important as they lay a foundation for the rest of a child's development and how they function throughout their life!

Brains

Infants are born with approximately 100 billion neurons in their brains (Ackerman 1992). While some connections are made before birth, most neural connections are formed in the years from birth to three. Imagine—100 billion! That's a huge amount of potential waiting to come together. In their first year, children's brains double in size. By age three, the brain is 80 percent of its adult size, and by age five, 90 percent (Dekaban and Sadowsky 1978; Lenroot and Giedd 2006). According to the Center on the Developing Child at Harvard University (2018), "more than 1 million new neural connections form every second" in a young child's brain. All this offers us as parents an awesome opportunity—and responsibility—to provide optimal experiences for our child's learning, growth and development, to help her thrive during this incredible time.

Shatz (1992) writes that neurons that "fire together, wire together" (p.64)—that is, when repeated or meaningful experiences cause neurons to fire, those neurons begin to "wire together," or form networks. What this means is that the experiences children have in the early years have a significant impact on their building neural connections and networks. The experiences that young children have, in response to both positive and negative events, affect the developing architecture of their brains as they move towards independence.

RESEARCH SHOWS

Research by Hyde et al. (2009) shows that music can actually change the size and speed of our brains! In one study, six-year-old children who received 15 months of musical training showed increased brain size and speed in their motor and auditory processing areas; compared to control groups, the music class group's brains grew bigger and processed faster. And the benefits to a child's brain from early childhood music training are long lasting. Research by Skoe and Kraus (2012) suggests that these changes are maintained into adulthood even when the children didn't continue music lessons into adulthood.

Minds and bodies

In addition to the development of neural connections and networks, daily experiences also directly influence the development of children's minds and bodies. It is through these early experiences that children form a sense of who they are as individuals. A wide range of self-skills are impacted by experiences, including self-esteem, self-worth, self-confidence, self-efficacy and the curiosity to explore. Basically, experiences help shape how children feel about and value themselves, their ability and confidence to learn new things, their belief in their power to have an effect on others, and their ability to learn and form relationships.

Experiences affect almost every aspect of a child's daily life: the ability to go to sleep at night, to manage difficult feelings and stress, to focus and maintain attention, and to develop problem-solving skills. Experiences affect children's ability to play nicely with others and make friends. Experiences affect the development and health of their bodies. Experiences affect their ability to function successfully when they enter elementary school. Experiences affect the formation of their cultural identity and their ability to appreciate the diversity of other cultures.

The experiences children have, in interaction with their genetic inheritance and biology, have a direct impact on how they function and develop on a daily basis and on who they will become as adults.

What experiences matter most?

Almost every experience that a child has informs the way he will develop, the growth—cognitive, physical, social and emotional—that she will enjoy. But some experiences have a particularly serious impact. While each area in this next section will be explored in depth in the proceeding chapters, both in terms of general development and how music can have an impact, below is an overview to give you a sense of how the puzzle of development fits together.

Responsive relationships

Quality early relationships are ones in which we respond to our child's needs consistently, compassionately and within a reasonable amount of time. Chapter 2 takes a closer look at how children need support from the adults in their lives to help them both meet their needs on a daily basis and develop the ability to manage, control, understand and express their needs independently. Research by Farrell *et al.* (2016) suggests that parenting environments that mitigate high stress produce healthier outcomes for children. When children grow up in an environment where their needs are met relatively consistently, predictably and compassionately, they will more likely develop neural pathways that support a view that the world is a safe place and that needs can and will be met.

Through our responding to our child's needs consistently, compassionately and predictably:

- children can learn that stress is tolerable and can be managed

- they will more likely learn to better manage frustration and control their impulses more readily, and develop the confidence and ability to regulate their own thoughts, feelings and bodies

- they will be better able to live and work with others more cooperatively

- they will be more likely to learn to express and communicate their needs in more goal-directed ways.

On the other hand, when needs are met inconsistently, chaotically or even violently, children can develop a negative reaction to managing their needs, be less able to regulate their feelings, thoughts and bodies and feel less trusting and safe towards others. Stress may be experienced as overwhelming and intolerable. This can result in social, emotional, behavioral, learning and physical challenges (Shonkoff *et al.* 2012).

Sensory input and opportunities to learn cause-and-effect relationships

In addition to responsive relationships, children also benefit from experiences in which they have enough quality sensory input and opportunities to physically act on what they are seeing, hearing, touching and smelling. They need to use their bodies to explore and play, in order to figure out cause-and-effect relationships through active exploration. They need us to provide experiences which help foster and encourage their innate curiosity and use their active imaginations.

As they grow and develop, young children need opportunities to play, both on their own and with other children. When children engage their bodies and imaginations through play, they are building their brains, minds and bodies. They are gathering information. They are analyzing what they come in contact with—places, objects, people—as they learn to solve more complex problems. This is their job! They are exploring social roles in order to figure out who they are and how to get along with others. They are building their skills to move in and out of different social situations more flexibly.

Children also need experiences that allow them to practice skills they've mastered and to learn new skills that are just beyond their reach. Mastery is a great motivator for children to explore, learn and grow. As they are learning, children need us to know when to step in and show them and when to step back and let them try on their own. They often need to learn on their own more than they need us to teach them. But they do need to know that we're here to help and teach them should they need us.

Neuroplasticity

Now, I am definitely not saying that children who are developing atypically or who have difficulty managing their feelings, needs, behavior, relationships, bodies or focus and attention have had negative childhoods, bad parenting or not enough quality developmental experiences. There are many factors that contribute to how a child functions in different circumstances in addition to how we parent, including their temperament and biological inheritance, illness and injury and other experiences outside of our control.

But because of our brain's neuroplasticity (the term for the ability of its neurons to change and physically wire and re-wire based on experience), children who have difficulties managing a particular task or aspect of development, who have special needs, who are developing atypically or have suffered injury, trauma or illness, have the potential to learn new ways to cope with challenges. They can build new skills when they are provided with optimal learning experiences that help them build new neural pathways or reroute current pathways. Cramer *et al.* (2011) write about the brain's ability to change based on experience.

It is up to us as parents and professionals to provide responsive relationships, healthy multi-sensory experiences and quality opportunities to play and physically work on their environments, build skills and gather information, through which our children can develop, and form neural pathways that support healthy development. It is up to us to know, understand and treat our children as individuals with unique skills, abilities and challenges within the frame of general development as we help them learn new skills and develop new abilities.

So, how can we best provide our infants, toddlers and preschoolers with optimal experiences?

Music matters

Music provides the best of all worlds for young children's learning and growth in all areas of development. During the early years of rapid development, music powerfully and joyfully offers opportunities for children to develop their brains, minds, bodies, relationships and cultural identities. It's at the top of the list. Music is the Mt. Everest of healthy experiences for young children. It's the cream of the crop. On a scale of 1–10, it's an 11! Am I being emphatic enough? Music matters.

Music and responsive relationships

As covered in depth in Chapter 2, music is an incredibly powerful way for adults to bond with their child, student or patient. Music helps build the intimate, safe and trusting responsive relationships with young children described above, which are foundations for forming future healthy relationships. Music is a great way to show and share love. As music is primarily an emotional form of communication, we can use it to respond to the needs of a child outside of the limits and challenges of spoken language. We can even use singing to connect and form relationships with our children even before they're born (hearing develops prenatally, in the fifth or sixth month). Research shows that children actually form a connection to their mother's voice prenatally and can remember songs they hear in utero.

RESEARCH SHOWS

In one study by Partanen *et al.* (2013), four-month-old infants demonstrated memory of music they heard at 29 weeks in utero, and numerous studies, including Kisilevsky *et al.* (2003), have shown that infants in utero recognize their mothers' voices. It appears that, before birth, a child's brain is developing neural pathways for bonding through sound. This builds a strong case for using music in general, and specifically singing, both before and after birth, to foster a healthy connection.

Particularly salient to the power of music in the early years is that it can help foster emotional connections with infants who have yet to develop language, with toddlers and preschoolers who are just learning to master language, and with children with language and communication challenges. Singing together can help promote social bonding and help us feel more connected to each other. As discussed in Chapter 3, play songs are embedded with social skills lessons that help children develop social confidence, competence and the ability to move more flexibly between social situations and make friends.

On a biological level, research by Kreutz (2014) and Keeler *et al.* (2015) shows that when people sing together the social bonding hormone oxytocin is released in higher quantities. In addition, stress levels and the experience of negative feelings are reduced when we sing, as compared to when we are just talking. Just imagine the social bonding you can do on long car trips by singing together!

Music can also serve as a transitional aid, like a stuffed animal or security blanket, as children move from parental relationships to a larger world. I find this aspect of music to be particularly powerful and beautiful—that having specific songs that you and your child share can serve as powerful and intimate symbolic reminders of you and your child's shared love and relationship. These songs can provide security and reassurance and help build resilience. Children often remember and cherish the songs sung together during the early years for the rest of their lives. My wife still tears up whenever she hears "The Fox"; this was a song that her family, especially her father, would sing as she was growing up. These songs are powerful symbolic representations and reminders of a shared relationship and love.

Music and sense of self

Chapter 2 also provides examples on how to use music, through how we bond, to help children develop a positive sense of who they are, what they can do and a sense of themselves as separate from others as they build their self-esteem, self-worth, self-efficacy and self-confidence. The love we give our children through holding and singing to them, or actively listening to them sing to us, is an opportunity to help them feel loved and cared for just for who they are as they develop their self-esteem. An infant seeing the positive reaction she gets from others when she bangs a drum is building the sense that she is a unique and important person separate from others, and that she has the power to have a positive effect on others, a component of self-efficacy.

Music can help children develop feelings of self-worth and confidence as individuals as well as of members of a group. A preschooler singing with a group of classmates or with his family can increase his feelings of acceptance as a valued member of a group.

A toddler mastering the hand movements to "The Wheels on the Bus" (Ch. 3) can feel a tremendous sense of accomplishment, which can in turn fuel confidence to try to learn new things.

As discussed in Chapter 3, music is an inclusive activity. Singing, playing instruments, dancing, listening and hearing live music together all offer opportunities for children and adults with a wide range of skills, abilities and ages to participate together. Even infants can feel that they are an important part of a group by shaking their rattles while the rest of the family sings a rousing round of "Row Your Boat." A family or classroom with varied abilities and skills that engages in circle dances together is building a sense of community through successful engagement in synchronized movement. I have found that multi-generational music groups provide immense benefit to all involved, from infants to great-grandparents.

Music, big feelings and self-regulation

Chapter 7 covers how music can help children learn to manage their feelings, thoughts and bodies. From anger to anxiety to meltdowns to difficulty with transitions or trying new things, music can help children learn to cope with big feelings and ways to manage their behavior. We can use music to calm, energize, relieve boredom and focus or redirect attention. Songs can help challenge erroneous thought patterns that lead to anxiety.

We can sing, hold and dance with our child as we join with the rhythm of his mood. We can then slowly modulate, or change, the rhythm in order to help him change his mood, calm or energize his body, co-regulate his feelings, and redirect his attention. And we can use music to help our child regulate when in close proximity, by holding our child, or when we're singing to her from across the room. We can use music to reassure by letting her know we are close by.

In addition to specific songs, games and activities that help children build skills, the actual expressive elements of music, including volume, speed, timbre and articulation, are not random or abstract. Loud, soft, fast, slow, short and long, to give a few examples, mimic the emotional and physical characteristics of human expression. They can help children learn ways to express themselves both within and outside of music. Through mastering and practicing these skills in music, children can learn effective ways to communicate and express themselves in other situations as well.

RESEARCH SHOWS

Music can help increase children's ability to regulate their feelings. In one study by Corbeil, Trehub and Peretz (2016), infants exposed to infant directed singing (basically singing with prolonged vowel sounds, exaggerated pitches and repeated phrases) were slower to express distress. It seemed that the singing helped them maintain a calm state for a longer period of time than control groups, who were exposed to infant directed speech and adult directed speech but no singing.

Lullabies and play songs

Lullabies are great examples of songs that can help children relax and calm their minds, thoughts and bodies through slow repetitive sounds, usually with lower volume and smaller melodic steps. Lullabies can help parents manage bedtime more easily, and help children develop good sleep hygiene as they learn to independently soothe themselves to sleep. Some of my favorite lullabies are the American folk song "Hush Little Baby" (Ch. 4) and "Coqui" from Puerto Rico. Singing slow songs and holding and rocking to a progressively slower rhythm can help children lower their heart rates, calm their minds and help them remember how much they are loved.

As we'll examine in Chapter 4, when included as part of bedtime routines music can also help children learn what's expected of them, as well as viscerally help move them into "sleep mode" through their associations to their favorite bedtime songs. While not a lullaby, Raffi's "Brush Your Teeth" song is a fun song to help get children in the mood to start preparing for bed with some teeth cleaning.

On the other side of the energy spectrum, Chapter 7 explores how play songs can help children energize, increase their focus and attention, and learn to control and coordinate their bodies. Chapter 3 provides many examples on how to use play songs to help children learn to work together and build their social-emotional skills. For example, the traditional American children's song "Bluebird" (Ch. 3) helps children learn to take turns and follow simple directions. The "bluebird" child flies through the window created by the rest of the children who are holding hands in a circle. Each child has to wait his or her turn to be the "bluebird," while the others work together to open and close their windows by raising and lowering their arms. "Obwisana" (Ch. 3) is a passing game play song from Ghana that helps children learn to focus and cooperate through coordinating their movements in a group. The children have to keep a steady beat while passing objects around the circle.

Music as a multi-sensory playground

From sounds to visuals to textures to the feelings of their bodies moving, music is a multi-sensory playground for young children; it offers rich sensory input to hungry brains. Children learn from what they hear, touch, feel and see. Whenever children act on the rich sensory input they are receiving, adapt their actions, figure out patterns and sequences, and learn which things go together and how things work, they are building new skills and abilities.

- Through the simplest of actions—being held and rocked to a steady beat—children are learning to orient their bodies based on what they hear, see and feel.

- Through independently dancing and moving to music, children are getting rich auditory, visual and physical input; they learn to control and coordinate their bodies as they move through space.

- Through manipulating musical instruments with their hands and mouths, children are learning to coordinate their senses with their bodies. They are figuring out the relationships between what they hear, feel and see and how, through their movements, the sound was produced.

- When children sing, they are playfully learning to coordinate the many muscles in their mouths through the sounds they hear themselves make.

- When they shake a rattle, hear the sound and see how others react, they are building a sense of cause and effect.

- When they learn to play a familiar melody on a xylophone or keyboard, they are engaging in purposeful movement as they learn to coordinate their senses with action and thought.

Through musical stimulation, children can learn to listen more attentively, focus their hearing, discriminate different sounds in their environment, and increase their ability to figure out where the sounds are coming from. Musical experiences can help children improve their ability to make sense of and process what they are hearing. Music can help children build their internal library of sounds as they learn to associate sounds with the things that make those sounds. As they listen to live and recorded music, children can learn to identify different instruments just by the sounds they produce. They can learn to focus on one sound from a field of other sounds. "Musical instrument bingo" (Ch. 6) is a great activity to help build the ability to discriminate what they are hearing and focus their hearing.

Music, language and communication

As discussed in Chapter 6, when children hear songs and engage in singing activities, they are developing their language and communication skills during the critical period of language development. A parent singing silly sounds back and forth with his preverbal infant in a playful, conversation-like manner is helping establish the building blocks of speech, language and communication, in addition to bonding and connecting with his child.

Children learning simple songs and singing them over and over and over and over again are doing important speech and language work. They are developing their ability to coordinate the muscles in their mouth, building their vocabularies, learning the melody, or prosody, of speech, and learning the rhythm of how words go together, all while developing a positive attitude towards words and language.

RESEARCH SHOWS

The songs we choose in the early years are important. Infants show a preference for "infant directed singing" as opposed to "adult directed singing." In one study, Masataka (1999) showed that two-day-old infants showed increased attention when exposed to children's play songs vs. adult music.

Music and cognition, or learning

Chapter 6 also goes into depth as to how music can help young children gather information, learn new concepts and categories of objects, develop their creativity and learn problem-solving skills, all of which helps them both to prepare for the transition to elementary school and to build a foundation for a lifetime of learning. There are many songs that help children learn specific information such as numbers, letters, shapes, colors, seasons, transportation, community members and more as they build their cognitive skills.

- "Old MacDonald" (Ch. 6) is one of the most popular songs that help children learn to pair an animal with the sound it makes.

- There are many counting up and down songs, including "Five Little Ducks," "Five Green and Speckled Frogs" (Ch. 6), "1, 2, Buckle My Shoe" (Ch. 6) and "Five Little Monkeys Jumping on the Bed" (Ch. 5).

- "Jenny Jenkins" (Ch. 6) is a great song to learn about colors.

- "Ain't No Bugs" (Ch. 6) teaches about bugs along with building rhyming skills.

Songs to teach social skills

The rhythm, melody, rhyming, repetition and feelings generated by music help children store and retrieve memories, facilitating their learning and remembering of the concepts presented in the songs. With my childhood friend, award-winning author, clinical psychologist and excellent drummer, Jed Baker, PhD, I co-wrote an album called "Be a Friend: 16 Songs to Teach Social Skills." Some of his approaches to managing big feelings are explored in Chapter 7. The idea of the social skills lessons album was that hearing and repetitively singing these fun songs, with catchy melodies, rhythms and rhymes, would reinforce previously learned social skills, teach new skills and help the concepts become more deeply remembered and used.

And music is a way for children to learn across multiple domains simultaneously (Parlakian and Lerner 2010). It provides opportunities to develop a variety of skills within one activity. For example, a preschooler doing a "freeze dance" is learning about the social skill of personal space, while they are learning to control their bodies on cue, while they are building physical stamina, while they are building their auditory processing skills through listening and responding to cues, while they are building their memory through learning the lyrics of the song, while they are building their speech skills through singing the song.

RESEARCH SHOWS

Sridharan *et al.* (2007) used sophisticated brain scans (functional magnetic resonance imaging scans (fMRI)) to show that music activates attentional and anticipation areas of our brains. This has implications for a child learning new information and skills. Music can help them focus longer, build an understanding of patterns and relationships in the world and thus improve memory for what they are experiencing.

Research by Woodruff Carr *et al.* (2014) also suggests that a child's ability to synchronize to a steady beat can help predict reading readiness skills later in childhood. The researchers used a child's ability to match a beat through drumming as an assessment tool in children as young as three for identifying potential problems developing literacy skills later in elementary school. Their conclusion was that the ability to hear and process sounds in our heads is related to our ability to use spoken and written language and is predictive of our ability to read in elementary school.

Music and physical development

Chapter 5 explores ways to use music to help young bodies build strength, coordination, balance, awareness and stamina. "Head, Shoulders, Knees and Toes" (Ch. 5) is both a fun and an important way for children to develop awareness of their body parts, to enhance coordination by moving in rhythm, and to build strength of their core muscles in order to develop the ability to walk, run, jump and move more independently. A child learning to move his fingers while singing "Itsy Bitsy Spider" (Ch. 5) is developing the fine motor skills of coordinating individual fingers to perform different actions which help tell a story.

These physical skills are helpful in learning to play music, but they are also transferable, as children get older, to writing, using computers, manipulating objects, making art, and eventually to any number of jobs that require fine motor skills. And, physical development is part of a dynamic system that is integrated with all areas of development. One of my close elementary school friends, with whom I took saxophone lessons in elementary school, and who was a great bass player in high school, is now a brain surgeon! Coincidence? Maybe not!

Music and understanding culture

As explored in Chapter 8, learning music that is important to their families and communities as well as music from around the world can help children both learn about their own culture and develop an appreciation of the diversity of human cultures. Through inclusive music-making, children can learn to see similarities and differences as qualities to learn about each other—rather than in terms of "greater than or less than." I still remember how my sixth grade teacher, Ms. Croneheim, played the South African singer Miriam Makeba's recording of "Pata Pata" for our class as a way to help us learn about South African culture. We traveled, through music, to another country, another culture—and we learned to appreciate it. That song still gets me moving to the beat! And my best friend from elementary school still shares this memory with me. Whenever we hear this song, we are transported to another time and place. Music helped deeply encode this shared memory, and song, in our brains.

Getting started with a music area

Set up a "music area" in your home, classroom or therapy room in which your child can play music alone, with you and with her friends. Provide instruments and musical props for her to use that are child friendly and safe. You may also want to provide a music player for him to use. You will find many different songs, games and activities in the following pages that you can try at home in which you can incorporate the instruments listed below.

Support both structured and unstructured music time. Sometimes try teaching a new song and other times encourage free musical play and exploration. Direct your child towards the music area when they are having big feelings as well as during playdates or when bored.

Note: Read the manufacturer's warning labels about age-appropriateness for each instrument as some contain small or pointy parts that are not safe for children under three years old. Also, know your individual child and what is most safe and fun for them. I do not recommend providing headphones for young children as you will want to monitor what and how they are listening. Headphones at too high a volume can damage their hearing.

Suggested list of instruments and props for your "music area":

- maracas and egg shakers
- drums with and without mallets and sticks
- tambourines
- rain sticks
- triangles
- rhythm sticks
- sand blocks
- xylophone and mallets
- ukulele or child-size guitar
- scarves
- play parachute.

Putting it all together

When we intentionally, purposefully and constructively engage in musical experiences with our children, we are helping them engage all areas of their brains as they build important neural connections and networks. Through music we can help them learn across all domains of development simultaneously. Music provides powerful opportunities for sharing love and forming important responsive relationships with our young children, providing rich multi-sensory stimulation, and allowing them to gather information, learn about cause-and-effect relationships, and build a wide variety of skills. They will be learning as children are meant to learn, through using their imaginations and active physical play.

Just to be clear, when I write that music can help your child's development, I don't mean that putting on a recording of Mozart every morning will help their brains grow and will result in higher SAT scores. That popular misconception has been debunked. Music is not something that you can apply to fix a problem.

What music offers is basically a multi-sensory gym for a child's brain, mind and body. Through providing healthy musical experiences, we are helping build a solid foundation for optimal growth throughout our children's lives. As we've discussed above, research confirms all of this, showing us that music can have a powerful effect on children's brains, even before they're born, and the effects of musical experiences in childhood last well into adulthood.

Music is not magic

Music, however, isn't magic. I don't want to appear like an old-fashioned snake oil salesman presenting a cure-all substance that can fix whatever ails you. Music isn't going to be the magical cure for every developmental challenge, issue, injury or disorder. Music isn't something you can "apply" to fix a problem. It's a process—a deeply meaningful, effective and powerful process that can enhance every facet of your child's development—and that can provide tremendous satisfaction to you as a parent.

2

BONDING THROUGH MUSIC

Building a Safe, Secure and Loving Connection with Your Infant, Toddler or Preschooler

When a young child enters our lives, through birth or adoption, as a babysitting charge, or as a student, client or patient, the first and most important thing we want is for them to feel safe, secure and loved. We do this because we care. We care because of something John Bowlby (1969) called attachment. It's important. We have an innate drive to attach to, bond with, connect to and take care of the special children in our lives. Bonding matters.

Children also have a drive to connect, bond with and attach to the special adults in their lives. Throughout the early years, children need the adults in their lives, starting with their parents, to keep them safe, meet their needs and show them love.

The incredible drive to attach between children and adults makes sense. Infants, toddlers and preschoolers are all vulnerable. The development of their physical bodies and brains takes a long time. They need the adults in their lives to protect them and to help them survive and manage their needs on a daily basis. They need the important adults in their lives on the long journey to becoming independent adults, to help them form a sense of who they are, build skills, gather information and build a foundation for their future development.

The bond we make with our children is built around our meeting their needs responsively—that is, how quickly, consistently, predictably and compassionately we respond to their needs as they arise.

As introduced in Chapter 1, it is through our meeting their needs responsively that young children learn how to manage and regulate their needs on their own. They learn that moods can change, hunger can be satisfied, anger can dissipate, and interests can be engaged and boredom relieved. It is through these early relationships that children build their first social connections and start building their social networks, develop their attitudes about people, and learn the rules of their social worlds.

It is from their early relationships that children learn that they are lovable for who they are. It sounds like a platitude, but it's true. Their experience of being loved provides the foundation of self-esteem. Their experience of loving others provides joy. Learning that they can have a positive effect on others and that they have the power to influence their environment builds feelings of self-efficacy. Learning that they are capable of learning new things builds self-confidence.

In addition to meeting their physical survival needs and encouraging a positive sense of self, a healthy attachment and responsive relationship can help children feel more secure, confident and eager to follow their innate curiosity. Remember from Chapter 1 that young children's brains and minds are "experience-dependent." They need enough quality relationships and sensory and motor experiences to allow them to form healthy neural connections and networks. Secure bonding helps children feel secure and confident as they explore and act on their worlds and learn how things work. How we attach with our children can directly impact their brain development.

Children whose needs are met more responsively are more likely to be open to and interested in using their senses to interact with, gather information from and learn about the wider world. Children whose needs are met responsively will be more likely to develop a more positive attitude about their ability to learn new things. This can help them to more fully develop their imaginations, problem-solving abilities and critical thinking skills. They will more likely feel secure to follow where curiosity takes them. A child's curiosity is a powerful developmental driver!

Development is a lengthy and slow process; healthy attachments through safe and trusting responsive relationships are important throughout childhood, not just when children are infants. Toddlers and preschoolers also need a safe base to return to after exploring and expressing their independence. My kids are almost grown and I feel the attachment as strong as ever!

Young children need safe, trusting, loving relationships in order to build their brains, minds and bodies—to become, in other words, their best selves.

Music is uniquely made for bonding

Music is uniquely suited to meeting both a child's and a parent's, caregiver's or professional's need for attachment. Through a relationship built on music, we can help our children feel safe, secure and loved. Through music, we can help them learn to manage their feelings, bodies and thoughts.

We can respond to our children's needs through music, whether up close, holding them in our arms, or from across the room. We can use music to help them learn strategies and tools to manage their needs on their own. Through a relationship built on music, we can help our child develop a sense of herself as a unique and lovable individual who is capable of learning new things. Through music, we can help our child engage his curiosity and confidence to explore his world, gather information and build skills as he learns how things work.

Early relationships built through music can be enduring, intimate and meaningful.

Love and connection

Music is made for giving and receiving love. This capacity starts early. As we mentioned in Chapter 1, research shows that children can differentiate their mother's voice from a stranger's voice prenatally. Even before they're born, children use sound and music to figure out and connect with individuals who are safe and are designated to take care of them. This has huge implications for the use of singing in order to bond in early childhood. Music has all the ingredients for the bonding recipe. Singing to your child while holding and looking at them is a wonderful way to connect and share love. Listening to your child sing, either the lyrics to a simple song or musical babble, helps your child feel your relationship, and learn that they have the ability to give love as well as receive it.

Communication

Music is perfectly designed to connect and communicate with children who are preverbal, who are just beginning to master language, or who have language and communication challenges. Music can convey emotion and increase attention without using language, to help connect with and focus young children.

When we respond to our hungry or fussy baby by singing with slow, exaggerated vowel sounds, exaggerated expression and repeated words and phrases (probably, without realizing it, using a technique called "infant directed singing" or IDS), we are focusing their attention, helping them regulate themselves, and showing that we care. We are also providing them with sensory stimulation in order to build an internal library of the sounds of their native language.

Infant directed singing

Researchers have found that parents, caregivers and siblings throughout the world instinctively and spontaneously communicate with young children by singing slowly, at a higher than normal pitch, and with exaggerated emotional expressiveness—a combination of qualities labeled infant directed singing, or IDS (Lewkowicz 1998; Trehub 2001; Trehub, Schellenberg and Hill 1997; Trehub and Trainor 1998; Trehub, Unyk and Trainor 1993). While IDS supports the development of early language skills, it is primarily a powerful way to help parents and children bond and communicate on a preverbal and emotional level. Through IDS, we are connecting with how our children are feeling, helping them change and modulate their moods, and increasing their attention. These are meaningful and important musical moments.

The universality of IDS, along with its benefit to both parents and children from before birth, strongly supports the argument that it evolved to benefit human survival—as a way to help children survive and develop optimally (Huron 2003).

Sandra Trehub (2001) writes that mothers tend to change their singing styles as their children grow, in response to their perceptual abilities and needs: parents use higher pitches and more slurred tones when singing to infants than they do when singing to preschool-age children, and mothers show a remarkable consistency of tempo and pitch when singing the same songs to their young children but on different occasions. These "ritualized" aspects of their singing may help their voices and the songs they sing become more recognizable and memorable for infants, and the increased attention and focus produced from using IDS can lead to increased connection, bonding and communication (Trehub and Trainor 1998). The emotional quality of IDS and its ability to arouse, calm and convey emotions can help children begin to learn to regulate their own emotions.

These many benefits of IDS, including increased attention in children and maintenance of a strong emotional bond, may in turn have helped early human children sleep and feed more effectively, enhancing growth and an infant's potential to survive—and, as a result, humankind may have eventually developed a genetic predisposition to this musical form of communication (Trehub 2003).

As music therapy professor and researcher Shannon K. de l'Etoile (2006) suggests, "Essentially, ID singing provides an 'emotional grammar' through which mothers and infants can practice their most personal and meaningful interactions" (p.25).

Developing a sense of self through music

When our children experience joy from being held while we dance together to our favorite jam, they are learning that they are loved and lovable, which in turn builds their self-esteem. When we truly listen to our child haphazardly hitting their toy xylophone, we are showing we care. We are showing them that they are important and that their expressions matter. We are also helping them learn the social skill of listening, through our modeling.

When we respond enthusiastically to our child hitting a drum, they are learning that they are separate from us and that they have power to influence people in their world. They develop a sense of self-efficacy in learning that they are capable of affecting others positively. When we make music together with our children, integrating their sounds with ours, we are helping them build a sense of who they are as unique individuals and as members of a family.

When they learn to sing "star" at the end of our singing "Twinkle, twinkle little _____," they increase their confidence in their ability to learn more words to the song and to learn other songs. This can inspire them to try and learn new things.

As mentioned in Chapter 1, when we have a set of "our songs," songs that we always sing together, that are special to our relationship, we are creating a symbolic representation of our attachment and love. This library of songs can help our children feel safe and protected and serve as a reminder of the security that your relationship as a parent or caregiver provides. These songs can help function as a reminder of the shared love that children can keep with them at all times. This can help build resilience. The feelings these songs generate can last a lifetime as reminders of the special bond in a relationship. They can be sung in times of joy to celebrate and in times of sorrow to help ease emotional pain. Take a minute to think about songs that remind you of a special relationship or time in your life. Are there songs from your childhood, adolescence or courtships that instantly and physically bring back memories and feelings of those times?

Self-regulation

As we bond with our child and join in her music, connecting with her rhythms, melodies, volume and tempo, we are showing that we hear her and that she is not alone. As described in Chapter 1, we can then gradually modulate to a different tempo, volume and mood and try to help her modulate her thoughts, feelings and physical state as well. Lullabies are great examples of assisting our children in modulating to a slower, more relaxed rhythm as they approach bedtime. In contrast, "play songs" can help children energize and focus through movement and interaction with other children and adults.

When we help our children regulate themselves through music, either calming or energizing, they are learning that feelings and states can and do change in predictable and controllable ways. These are important first steps in their learning to manage and control their own feelings, bodies and minds.

Putting it all together

Connect with your child on an intimate level during everyday moments through music, in what could otherwise have been a mechanical interaction. When you sing about what you are doing, you are bonding while helping your child build skills and learn about her world. You're teaching language skills, supporting his understanding of cause-and-effect relationships, building attention, building social skills, and increasing problem-solving skills.

When we intentionally make music to connect, bond, listen and respond, we are building a relationship that is a blueprint for our children's future relationships and a foundation for future development and learning. When we truly make music with the focus on the process, not the product, we are being responsive in an intimate and developmentally important way. It is through this connection that children can develop a sense of themselves as capable, confident and valued and begin to learn to independently regulate their feelings, thoughts and bodies. We are providing essential multi-sensory stimulation and opportunities for growth and development.

SONGS, GAMES AND ACTIVITIES FOR BONDING

This section includes specific songs and musical activities that you can use to develop a healthy bond with your child. While most songs in this book can be used for forming a close trusting relationship, I find these to be particularly useful especially during the earliest of years.

The accompanying music and video files can be downloaded from www.jkp.com/voucher using the code BOOMESE.

PRENATAL MUSIC

Start the party early and begin bonding through music before birth!

Purpose

Prenatal music helps your baby begin to recognize and know your voice and provides a way to help you and your baby de-stress or energize. As children's hearing develops during the fifth month of pregnancy, singing to them after this point will help them bond with your voice.

How to

- **Sing simple songs.** Choose two or three simple children's songs that you enjoy, such as "Twinkle, Twinkle Little Star" (see below) or "Hush Little Baby" (Ch. 4). Sing the songs while focusing attention on your baby. Watch for movement, kicks or calmness in response. Take deep breaths when singing and use these moments for your own relaxation as well.

- **Energize to your favorite dance music.** Dance is a great way to connect with your baby and for you to get some exercise. Keep your movements calm and safe and follow any recommendations regarding movement and exercise you may have received from your doctor or midwife.

- **Calm down to your favorite relaxing music.** Stress management is important for you and your baby as your body and lifestyle change during pregnancy. Take some time out every day to close your eyes, breathe deeply and listen to your favorite slow, relaxing music.

👍 Personal reflections

Some of my favorite music for relaxation music includes jazz piano such as music by Bill Evans, classical music such as the "Bach Cello Suites," and new age music such as George Winston's "Winter into Spring."

What music helps you or your baby relax?

Notes

MEANINGFUL MUSICAL MOMENTS

Turn everyday chores and interactions with your child into opportunities for intimate connections and learning!

Purpose

Singing and dancing with your child during the simplest activity can help you bond and connect with your baby in addition to assisting them to build important skills. When we sing during a diaper change, we are holding our child's gaze for a prolonged period of time and helping her increase her ability to focus and attend. When we make eye contact and sing back and forth during nursing or feeding, we are helping our child build social and language skills. When we sing about the food we are cooking while our child sits in his highchair, he is learning about food and nutrition.

How to

- **Use infant directed singing strategies.** Make eye contact with your child while singing slowly; use exaggerated high and low pitches and exaggerated emotions. Repeat important words and phrases and exaggerate your facial expressions. Pay attention to which sounds and interactions your child responds. Make up songs about what you are doing. Sing about what you think your child is experiencing—for example, "You are waaaaaaatching me cooooooook the dinner. Waaaaaaatch as I chop, chop, chop the spinach, spinach, spinach."

- **Use simple songs.** Sing simple songs such as "Itsy Bitsy Spider" (see Ch. 5) or "Row Your Boat" while you are walking, giving your child a bath, or feeding him. Watch for what songs he responds to with eye contact, attention, smiles and movement. Build a set of your child's favorite songs. Every once in a while, add a new song to the set.

- **Create singing conversations.** Engage in singing conversations with your child while doing the simplest activity, such as folding laundry. These can include vocalizing simple sounds or using actual words. While she sits and watches you, sing a sound or word and wait for her to respond. When she does, either copy her sound or respond in a musical way with your voice, as if you were having a conversation. Try to capture the "back and forth" quality of an actual conversation with questions and statements, but in a more musical manner. This will help keep your child's attention for longer periods of time and help her learn the rhythm, melody and patterns of language and music as you bond.

- **Identify teachable moments.** Use meaningful musical moments to help your child learn about the objects, activities and people in your world. Try adapting familiar songs to sing about what you are doing—for example, sing the melody of "Itsy Bitsy Spider" but insert words about what you are currently doing, i.e. "The itsy bitsy bath brush is washing off your back/ Down came the water and washed off all the soap/ Out came the wash cloth and cleaned off all the suds/ then the itsy bitsy bath brush is washing off your nose…" (This song has the added benefit of helping children learn their body parts!) Receptive language develops before expressive language, so even if your child is not repeating what you are saying, he or she is beginning to learn and remember what you are singing about.

👍 Personal reflections

Making up a song can feel awkward at first, but you'll quickly forget about that when you see the reaction on your child's face. You may even develop a repertoire of "made-up songs" that you return to often. In my music therapy work, I have young clients who joyfully remember our "spontaneous song" weeks and sometimes even months after I made them up.

What are some of the meaningful musical moments you share with your child?

Notes

LISTENING IS LOVING

Listen to your infant babble, your toddler string together words, or your preschooler sing the same song over (and over and over) again—through listening, we show our children that they are important, and we model an important social skill.

Purpose

Listening to our children is a powerful way to bond and connect as we help them build self-esteem, regulate their needs and learn social skills. They are learning that they have value when we pay attention to them as they sing or play instruments for us. They can learn to regulate themselves through venting and expressing themselves while we receive and accept what they are doing. We are modeling for them how to maintain eye contact and actively listen.

How to

When your child is singing, playing an instrument or dancing, take time to listen and watch—put your phone away so you can give undivided attention. Make comments on the *process* of what they are doing—for example, "I noticed that you had a very loud section followed by a softer section"—rather than focusing on the quality of their singing, dancing or instrument playing. Take time each day to ask them to play music for you, so you can listen to and watch them. Or put on a recording and ask your child to sing, play or move along.

Personal reflections

Some of my favorite memories of my children are of their singing for us when they were very young. My family still melts when we think of when our preschool-age children sang "God Bless America," "You Are My Sunshine," and "Walking On Sunshine" for us. Not only were these wonderful opportunities for us to connect with them through listening but also fond memories in the making.

What are some of your favorite listening moments?

Notes

PERSONAL SONG LIBRARY

Bond and connect with your child through building a library of songs that are "your songs."

Purpose

Use songs to build a symbolic reminder of your relationship and love. These songs will hold their intimate meaning for your entire lives. Your child can remember these songs when she needs soothing and help building resilience. Songs in your library can include traditional children's songs, adaptations of these songs, made-up new songs or popular favorites.

How to

Consistently sing specific songs that you and your child enjoy as part of your daily routines; identify collections of "car trip songs," "bedtime songs," "going to preschool" songs, and so on. Keep track of these songs by keeping a list on your phone or writing them in the "Notes" section below. While I don't advocate constantly videotaping every intimate musical moment, try preserving a video version of you and your child singing each song.

👍 Personal reflections

I used to sing "Hush Little Baby" for my children at bedtime when they were infants. It's one of my favorite songs, because it still holds that special feeling whenever I sing it. It transports me back to that memorable time.

What are the songs in your and your child's "personal song library"?

Notes

PLAY SONGS

Play songs can be used for connecting and bonding—and they are also just good plain fun!

Purpose

Connect with your child through active play. Play songs create a familiar structure within which you and your child can share time together. Your child will enjoy singing and dancing with you and will cherish these playful moments.

Note: I have included several sitting play songs here which are traditionally geared toward infants (although they can also be used with slightly older children). Play songs for older children and dance-oriented play songs are included in Chapters 3 and 5.

How to

Follow the directions for each specific song. For some you will sit facing each other, others with your child sitting in your lap, or with the two of you sitting side by side. As Professor John M. Feierabend (2006) recommends, try a variety of approaches to singing, including singing these for your children, encouraging your children to sing them for you, or singing them together. For added fun and engagement, try exaggerating the "payoff" of the songs—pause just before the last line of the song and wait for your child to provide it.

What play songs do you use to connect and bond with your child?

Notes

"Ride Away to Boston"

Traditional

I've heard many variations of this song. Some say "trot, trot to Boston" and "trit, trot to Boston," while others use the lyrics below.

Try singing this song by:

- holding your infant or toddler on your lap, either facing you or facing out, and gently bounce him up and down as if riding on a horse

- chanting the song slowly with an even beat

- opening your legs on the last word, "in," while holding your child's sides so they drop down a little between your legs. Make sure to hold on to her so she doesn't actually drop to the floor!

Ride away to Boston
Ride away to Lynn
Better watch out or you
Might fall in

"Open, Shut Them"

Traditional

This is another song that I have heard variations of. Face your child and open and close your hands as you begin chanting. Follow the movements as listed on the right side of the song. Try to maintain eye contact with your child as you sing. You should:

- face your child and open and close your hands as you chant

- follow the movements

- maintain eye contact with your child as you chant and move.

Open, shut them, open, shut them	*[open and close both hands at same time]*
Give a little clap, clap, clap	*[clap hands on the words "clap, clap, clap"]*
Open, shut them, open, shut them	*[open and close both hands at same time]*
Put them in your lap, lap, lap	*[put hands in lap]*
Creep them, creep them	*[crawl fingers up child's body]*
Creep them, creep them	

Right up to your chin, chin, chin	[stop at their chin]
Open up your little mouth	[open your mouth]
but do not let them in	[quickly put hands behind your back]

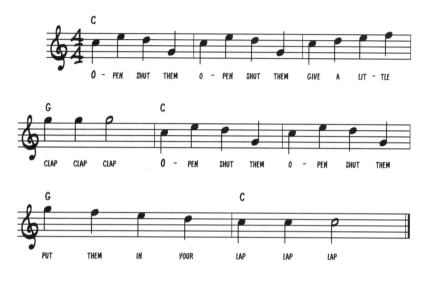

VERSE 2:
CREEP THEM CREEP THEM
CREEP THEM CREEP THEM
RIGHT UP TO YOUR CHIN CHIN CHIN
OPEN UP YOUR LITTLE MOUTH BUT
DO NOT LET THEM IN

"Twinkle, Twinkle Little Star"

Traditional

"Twinkle, Twinkle Little Star" is one of the most popular children's songs with the young children that I work with. It is great for bonding as well as for language and fine motor development.

- Sit facing each other.

- Sing the song for your child while engaging in the hand movements.

- Try leaving off the last word of each line; wait for your child to fill it in.

- Don't correct imprecise articulation of the words; rather, when you sing, model the correct sounds, and provide reinforcement with a big smile for trying and getting close.

- Watch as your child tries the hand movements, and offer praise for the effort.

Twinkle, twinkle little star	*[open and close each hand over head in "twinkle" motion]*
How I wonder what you are	*[continue to open and close each hand in "twinkle" motion]*
Up above the world so high	*[above head, put index fingers together and thumbs together in a "diamond" shape]*
Like a diamond in the sky	*[continue to hold diamond shape overhead]*
Twinkle, twinkle little star	*[open and close each hand over head in "twinkle" motion]*
How I wonder what you are	*[continue to open and close each hand in "twinkle" motion]*

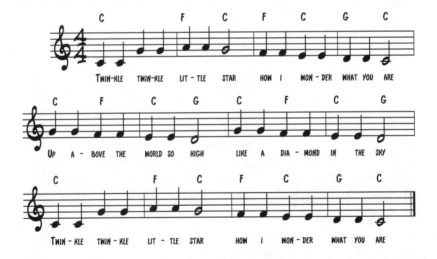

3

FRIENDS THROUGH MUSIC
Building Social-Emotional Skills—and Enjoying Playdates More!

As discussed in Chapter 2, a child's first relationships with the important adults in their lives, especially parents, are incredibly meaningful. They set the stage for future development and form a blueprint for future relationships. They help children develop their attitudes about themselves. It is from these relationships that they learn to trust their own sense of curiosity; play, explore and gather information through their senses; and figure out how things and people work.

As children enter the toddler and preschool years, however, they also become interested in forming relationships with their peers; they begin to play and learn from one another. They start to make friends.

Friends matter: The basics of children's social development

Friends are fun, but more than that, they help children learn, grow and develop. Friends help them learn to manage and cope with the many challenges of the early years and ultimately lead more fulfilling and meaningful lives. We are social beings. Our survival depends on our being able to live, work and get along with each other. It's important. We want our children to play nicely with others, learn to cooperate, and grow into caring, considerate adults. Friends matter.

We want our children to be able to:

- understand, express and manage their feelings in socially acceptable ways

- understand that others have ideas and feelings different from theirs

- easily adapt to new social situations

- make new friends.

During the early years, as their social networks expand, children start to form a sense of themselves as members of groups, including families, friends, preschool classes, communities and cultures. They continue to build their identities, but now also in relation to their family as well as this expanding network that includes their peers and community. These additional relationships inspire and require children to build more sophisticated and complex social-emotional skills. They are preparing to enter the more structured and socially complex environment of elementary school, and eventually adolescence and young adulthood, when they will lead more independent lives and rely more on their friends (as opposed to their parents) to get their needs met. These early relationships build a foundation for these future relationships.

Play

As children move through the early years, their play becomes more sophisticated and interactive. During the toddler years, they move from solitary to parallel play. During the later toddler and preschool years, children learn to play more interactively with each other and develop the awareness that others have thoughts, feelings and needs which can be different from their own. As you can imagine, and may remember, social-emotional skills and rules become more complex.

As their language develops, their imaginations bloom, and they begin to engage in pretend play. Children use play to explore the many roles and situations they see in the world around them. Their brains continue soaking up information from what they observe and what they are taught, as they try to figure out how all the social roles people engage in fit together, like pieces of a puzzle.

The future impact of social-emotional development

As you can imagine, learning social-emotional skills can help a child manage social situations more easily. It provides him with more options for how to understand and interact and thus provides more predictability when in a social situation. It also helps him move in and out of different social situations more confidently and resolve conflicts more easily. But a child's ability to manage her budding social-emotional life, or her social competence, can have a big impact on overall health and development throughout a child's life.

RESEARCH SHOWS

Social and emotional competence is a predictor of school success and even the ability to successfully navigate adulthood. Children who have the skills to manage their feelings and relationships with their peers and teachers are better prepared when they enter kindergarten. Researchers Moffitt *et al.* (2011) followed over 1000 children for 32 years and found that the ability to manage emotions, delay gratification and control impulses in childhood is related to a number of issues in adulthood: physical health, substance abuse, financial success and criminal history. A study by Jones *et al.* (2015) found that how well a child manages socially at age five is a predictor of how well that child will manage as an adult.

Social-emotional skills can be learned

While children have an innate drive to be social, the skills they need to accomplish that can be learned. A variety of factors affect how children develop social competency, including what they see, what they are taught, and the general emotional climate of their families (Morris *et al.* 2007). The primary ways that children learn social skills are observation and instruction. Many skills are internalized simply by watching the behavior of family and friends; we adults model social behavior, and our children learn from how we treat and interact with each other.

Children also learn through extrinsic experiences, including being taught a skill directly. As parents and caregivers, we can consciously *prepare* our children to enter social situations by teaching them specific skills and helping them learn ways to manage their feelings and needs. We can also coach them *during* social situations and help them learn while they are interacting in play and other social activities. And we can teach them *afterwards*, going over with them what behaviors were successful and providing ideas on things to try in the future.

Each child and family is unique. Some children benefit more from intrinsic learning—simply watching modeled behaviors—while others do better with direct teaching. And some skills are more readily internalized when presented explicitly, or when modeled. Most children learn from both methods depending on their personality, the context and the skill.

The overall emotional climate of a situation also affects what and how children learn. As we discussed in Chapter 1, experiences matter. Parenting styles and environments that take into account each child's individual temperament and learning style and that are more responsive to individual needs in calm, consistent and predictable ways help children learn social-emotional skills more optimally.

Music encourages the development of social and emotional skills

Music is an ideal activity for helping young children learn to play nicely with each other. Music is both a classroom for learning social-emotional skills and a real-life, everyday opportunity for building friendships—and having great playdates! Through music, we can help our children learn both intrinsically, through our modeling appropriate behaviors and their having opportunities to practice and experiment, and extrinsically, through our teaching and coaching, and we can create emotional climates that are conducive for building social-emotional skills.

There are many aspects of music that make it a particularly fun and effective way to help children build social-emotional skills and make friends. Let's look at four in particular:

- Music encourages emotional connections between those engaged in a musical activity.

- The learning of social-emotional skills is embedded in the structure of play songs.

- Music helps children learn perspective-taking—seeing the world from another's point of view.

- Knowing a shared or common set of songs can offer opportunities for instant connection and interaction with others and define relationships.

These aspects of music can help boost social confidence, build social-emotional competence, and enhance the quality of playdates. In short, music can help children have more fun while making close friends!

How music builds emotional connections

An important building block for making friends is building trust and forming an intimate emotional connection. When we feel a safe and trusting bond with someone, we are more likely to want to invest in a friendship with them. We are also more likely to be receptive to learning the skills necessary for making friends when the emotional climate is conducive to it.

There are several aspects of music that help foster this, including the biology of what happens during singing, the inclusive qualities of music-making, music's ability to help communicate on an emotional and non-verbal level, the ability to synchronize through joining rhythms and beats, and the intimacy felt from hearing music.

RESEARCH SHOWS

In terms of biology, research shows that making music together, specifically singing, has been shown to increase the release of the social bonding hormone oxytocin, and decrease the release of the stress hormone cortisol (Keeler *et al.* 2015; Kreutz 2014). Music-making has an actual physiological effect on our bodies, enhancing social connectedness.

The *inclusive quality* of music offers opportunities for people of all ages, abilities and cultures to build emotional connections with each other. Now, I am not talking about participating in a symphony orchestra and the skills needed for that! But play songs offer many opportunities for children with a wide range of skills and backgrounds to engage in a social activity together, to feel like they are valuable members of a group, and to build specific skills. When performing for families, I love watching an infant bob up and down to the rhythm of the music while sitting in a parent's lap, a toddler standing with legs wide and arms outstretched for balance, bouncing and rocking, and a preschooler pretending to be a frog and hopping up and down, all engaged together at the same time to the same song.

And speech and language skills are not a prerequisite, or requirement, for using music to connect, communicate and form a relationship. Music offers children who are preverbal or verbal, or who have language and communication challenges, opportunities to express themselves, connect emotionally and interact socially at the same time. A toddler tapping a tambourine during a structured group music-making experience is building a sense of being a member of a group; he can feel socially connected by adding his sound to the group's music. A preschooler with autism who has social and communication challenges, yet can jump like a monkey jumping on its bed with his classmates while listening to "Five Little Monkeys Jumping on the Bed," is engaging in a successful social experience and bonding with his peers, while learning to develop personal space skills of keeping an arm's length away from the other dancers.

Through music, we can connect with and show our understanding of how someone is feeling simply by joining in their rhythm and synchronizing with their beat or joining their melody when singing together. We may look at this as a symbolic connection, but it's actually real. We can truly connect and join with someone else through the act of music-making. This is as real as a relationship built through talking, playing together on the playground, in the classroom, or when playing a game together. I would say this might even be more intimate a relationship due to the emotional aspects of music discussed above!

And making music together is an incredibly intimate experience. When we hear music, it can sound and feel as if it's actually inside our heads and bodies. We can't shut it off. We can close our eyes when we don't want to see something, but we can't simply close our ears. When we hear music, it feels very close and personal. This can contribute to the bonds we feel with the people with whom we share musical experiences.

How play songs embed social-emotional skills lessons

Each play song is basically a mini social-emotional skills lesson. The actual structure of the songs and the actions embedded in the songs offer opportunities to practice previously learned skills and to learn new skills. These include, but are not limited to, making eye contact, maintaining and respecting personal space, controlling the volume of one's voice, taking turns, sharing, following directions, and perspective-taking. Play songs offer children opportunities to learn and practice how to play in a variety of ways including alone, in parallel and interactively.

From fingerplays to partner songs to passing games to circle dances to spontaneous unstructured musical play, children can learn many different skills and can transfer those skills to other social situations. Think about "The Hokey Pokey." As children "put their hand in, take their hand out, put their hand in and shake it all about," they are learning to listen, follow directions and coordinate their own movements with those of their friends. Those same skills can not only be transferred to other circle dances but also to the same dance in another setting. These skills can also be applied more widely, in basic social interactions.

When young children make music together, they are learning the rules of their social worlds. Whether it's the rules of a play song that instructs children on what to do at specific moments, or the rules of play in general in order for everyone to feel safe, happy and respected, play songs help children learn the value of balancing working together with getting their own needs met. They are building an internal sense of how to make friends and work together.

When a group of toddlers or preschoolers learns to dance fast and exuberantly and then "freeze" on command, they are learning to follow the rules of the song and to control their bodies, attention, focus and feelings. They are watching, learning and taking cues from each other. They are learning ways to have fun together while respecting the needs of all involved.

There is also a lot to be gained when children share their music with others. When they sing or play music for their friends, families or classmates, children are learning how to present themselves in a more public context. Self-esteem and confidence can be generated both from sharing what we have learned and from being listened to, acknowledged and respected. Children can also learn something else of value: the roles of performer and audience. I'm not a proponent of forcing children to perform for the benefit of adults, so I usually reframe the experience as "sharing" rather than "performing." This helps to focus more on the process than on the product of music-making.

Types of play songs that help children learn social-emotional skills

- **Fingerplays** are great parallel play songs for young children. (Parallel play, as most of you no doubt know, is when children play together but each is engaged in his or her own activity, often side-by-side, but with limited interaction between them.) Fingerplays involve using fingers, hands, arms and legs to act out different aspects of a story while singing or chanting. Children do their movements on their own but at the same time, while singing with each other, and there's no waiting for turns or having to coordinate activity with each other. Some of the more popular fingerplays are "Itsy Bitsy Spider" (Ch. 5), "The Wheels on the Bus" (Ch. 3) and "Twinkle, Twinkle Little Star" (Ch. 2).

- **Partner songs** help children learn to work together in pairs. Hand-clapping songs like "Pat-a-Cake" or "Miss Mary Mack" (both Ch. 3) are great partner songs; children have to coordinate movements with their hands while facing each other. Children learn to chant or sing while moving their hands in a variety of sequences while facing a partner. Partner dances, such as "Nabe, Nabe, Soku Nuke" or "Brother, Sister, Dance with Me" (both Ch. 3), help children learn to coordinate their entire bodies with a partner. Both hand-clapping and partner dances encourage children to make eye contact, follow directions, maintain control of their bodies, and work cooperatively.

- **Circle games and dances** help children learn to follow directions, work cooperatively in groups, and play more interactively. Passing games, such as "Obwisana" (Ch. 3) from Ghana, encourage children to learn to follow directions in a group as they sing and coordinate the passing of an object to the beat of the song. The satisfaction and joy children experience from working successfully as a group to achieve a shared goal often motivates them to learn the skills needed to work cooperatively. Skills learned in songs and dances like these include listening, following directions, maintaining control of one's body, respecting personal space, eye contact and taking turns. During play songs in general, but more often in interactive play songs, we also want to teach children how to complement, compromise and give feedback to each other without teasing. Play songs can be challenging to learn, and we want to help our children learn how to help each other learn rather than inhibit each other through negative feedback or teasing.

Simple **spontaneous unstructured musical play** is also a great way for children to learn how to make friends. It's important to provide time for free musical play where they can explore and experiment on their own. This type of play provides them with opportunities to practice their budding social-emotional skills. Try putting out a basket of age- and individually appropriate instruments and see what happens. You can do this while you are making dinner or during free play in your classroom. It's always a good idea to supervise to make sure children are playing safely.

On countless occasions during free musical play time, both with my own children and in my classes, I've observed one child spontaneously echo the rhythm of another child's drum beat. The face of the first drummer usually lights up and beams with surprise and joy at having their rhythm heard and copied. The feelings of power and delight and connection in being able to elicit a response from a peer is huge. Children often repeat the rhythm and wait for a response, just to confirm that it wasn't chance and that it was intentional, and to feel that power and delight again. As they continue, they often will vary the rhythm to see what happens next—will the response change to match their own beat? They are relating to each other and building their social competence through musical free play.

How music encourages perspective-taking

Through making music, children can learn that others may have different feelings from their own. Music can be used to help them learn to balance their needs with those of the group. For example, children can learn that when singing together in a group, it's important to use the same volume as their friends and not to sing too loudly or softly. They learn that they have to modulate their volume to fit with the group volume so that everyone is happy and can be heard—and so the music sounds good. Learning more interactive play songs necessitates their learning to manage many different feelings and ideas and having to regulate their behavior accordingly in order to all get along and successfully complete the tasks involved!

When children learn to take turns being the leader in an echo song or freeze dance, they are learning that not everyone can go first (or perhaps that some children actually don't want to go at all because they are hesitant about being singled out from the group). In order to successfully engage in these types of songs, each child has to learn to value and balance the needs, thoughts and feelings of others with their own. They can learn to understand, acknowledge and accept one another's perspective in tempering their responses and reactions.

Perspective-taking is an important and valuable social skill that can begin to be developed during the preschool years. Young children can learn to make room for others' needs as they expand their musical play. Through the shared "group identity" and bond that is created when truly making music together, children are often more receptive to learning that others have feelings and thoughts that might be different from their own. Music can present a common goal that motivates them to work together more interactively and cooperatively.

Through music, children can also learn how they are both similar to and different from their friends. They may notice that some children's voices sound different from theirs, or that they know different sets of songs and come from different musical cultures. (More about this in Chapter 8.) But through the joy experienced from musically playing and sharing together, they can learn to appreciate, rather than fear, their differences.

How shared songs help build connections and define friendships

As discussed in Chapter 2 in relation to forming a healthy attachment, having a shared set, or repertoire, of songs can help a child feel like they are a member of a group. It can increase their sense of belonging, as well as their confidence and competence. The set of songs provide a guide for how to play and socialize with their family and peers. It helps them feel more secure in being a part of something, increasing their feelings of connection with each other.

Learning songs that others know can help initiate a child into the surrounding social culture. It can help them build and define their social identity—with the added benefit of creating more enjoyable playdates.

Knowing songs from one's family or peer group can help children to more easily enter or move between different social contexts. Whether it's a playdate, a birthday party, a family function or preschool, knowing the same songs as the other children can help them feel more socially confident and competent. If they already know the play songs, they will more easily join in the game, such as of "Ring Around the Rosie" (Ch. 3), "The Wheels on the Bus" (Ch. 3) or "Nabe, Nabe, Soku Nuke" (Ch. 3). If others know the same songs as they do—songs like "If You're Happy and You Know It" (Ch. 3)—they can also more easily initiate musical play and have others more easily join them. Through a shared repertoire, the social "ice" will be more easily broken.

Children who enter preschool with knowledge of popular traditional children's songs will have social tools with which to immediately engage and interact with friends they haven't met yet. And once children learn the basic structure of circle dances like "Looby Loo" (Ch. 5), they can also begin to adapt the skills to learn new circle dances and make up their own variations, thus expanding their play.

In addition, knowing a common set of song structures, such as hand-clapping or circle dances, gives them a frame to anchor new musical and social-emotional skills. For example, learning to work with a partner and play the hand-clapping song "Miss Mary Mack" (Ch. 3) provides a basic structure into which they can "load" new partner songs such as "Brother, Sister, Dance with Me" (Ch. 3). Play songs have a common set of social-emotional rules: make eye contact, coordinate movements, listen, follow directions, maintain personal space, take turns, cooperate with a partner. Once these are learned, children can transfer these social-emotional skills to new songs and new social situations.

Putting it all together

From the preverbal infant, to the toddler grasping at her first words, to the preschooler who is beginning to engage interactively with his peers, to children who are developing atypically and those with challenges, music offers an abundance of opportunities to build social-emotional skills. If we truly want our children to learn how to make friends, we will provide them with opportunities to make music together. We will teach them songs and musical games that they can engage in with us and with their peers. We will help them learn the skills needed to sing, dance, play instruments and experience music together which they can use in music and other social situations.

"Ring Around the Rosie" is no joke. It's a graduate-level course for young children to learn how to live and work with others and build healthy relationships. According to the German anthropologists Sebastian Kirschner and Michael Tomasello (2010), "joint music making among 4-year-old children increases subsequent spontaneous cooperative and helpful behavior, relative to a carefully matched control condition with the same level of social and linguistic interaction but no music" (p.354). Simply speaking, it appears that music-making helps children to be more ready, willing and able to interact and play with each other in ways that help them make friends. That's pretty special!

SONGS, GAMES AND ACTIVITIES FOR MAKING FRIENDS AND DEVELOPING SOCIAL-EMOTIONAL SKILLS

This section includes specific songs and musical activities that you can use to support your child in learning a variety of social-emotional skills. The accompanying music and video files can be downloaded from www.jkp.com/voucher using the code BOOMESE.

Purpose

The songs in this section help children connect with their peers and other members of their communities while learning social rules and how to play nicely. They provide simple structures through which children can learn to interact with each other and make friends. The skills learned in play songs are transferable to other social situations. Through play songs, children can learn to balance their individual needs with those of the group.

How to

Preparing your children by teaching them specific songs, games and activities before playdates will help them feel more confident. And it's always useful to remind them about positive ways to play both before and during playdates—taking turns, sharing, and respecting personal space, for example.

Prepare your space for dance, movement and active play to make sure that there is nothing that children might hurt themselves on. Make sure that there's nothing that may fall down if children hop like frogs or jump around. Carpet, gym mats or grass are recommended surfaces to dance on as they are softer to land on in case someone falls.

Also, it's always a good idea to remind all young movers about keeping appropriate "personal space" while dancing. You can have them hold their arms outstretched to the front and sides and say this is how far you should be from each other when dancing and moving to music—unless, of course, the song calls for you to be closer, like holding hands.

FINGERPLAYS

It's time to sit with your child or a group of children on a playdate and engage in some parallel play with your fingers, hands, arms and legs! They will enjoy the time spent with you as well as have songs to play with their friends.

"Grandma's Glasses"

Traditional

Purpose

"Grandma's Glasses" is a chant that helps your child learn to control his body and calm himself as the chant ends with hands "folded gently in their lap." This is also a great fingerplay to use as a "transition song" when starting an activity, i.e. a meal or game, in order to get your child's attention and help him focus and control his body.

How to

Chant each line slowly, demonstrate the movement and wait for your child to copy you. Once your child learns each movement, then separately, slowly and with a steady beat try the entire chant. Try to chant at different speeds to increase engagement. You can also ask your child to chant it for you.

Here are grandma's glasses	[make circles with each thumb to index finger and hold over eyes]
Here is grandma's hat	[hold hands over head in triangle shape with point on top]
This is the way she folds her hands	[put one hand on top of the other in lap]
And lays them in her lap	

"The Wheels on the Bus"

Traditional

Purpose

In this favorite fingerplay, your child learns a basic structure in which to fill in different things and people that are "on the bus." They learn to move their arms to pretend they are doors, windows, wipers, horn, mommies, daddies and the driver. This is also a great song to help a child familiarize themselves with and thus increase their comfort with riding a school bus.

How to

Teach your child the song slowly while demonstrating the movements. Sometimes it helps to exaggerate the motions in order to help a child learn them. After they have learned the song, try asking "What's next on the bus?" and sing about that. You can also make up new things and people on the bus along with their accompanying motions.

The wheels on the bus go round and round	[roll arms in front of body]
round and round	[roll arms in front of body]
round and round	[roll arms in front of body]
The wheels on the bus go round and round	[roll arms in front of body]
All through the town	
★ ★ ★ ★ ★ ★	

cont.

The doors on the bus go open and shut	*[spread arms wide and bring hands together]*
open and shut	*[spread arms wide and bring hands together]*
open and shut	*[spread arms wide and bring hands together]*
The doors on the bus go open and shut	*[spread arms wide and bring hands together]*
All through the town	
★ ★ ★ ★ ★ ★	
The windows on the bus go up and down	*[raise arms over your head and then bring down to the floor]*
up and down	*[raise arms over your head and then bring down to the floor]*
up and down	*[raise arms over your head and then bring down to the floor]*
The windows on the bus go up and down	*[raise arms over your head and then bring down to the floor]*
All through the town	
★ ★ ★ ★ ★ ★	
The wipers on the bus go swish, swish, swish	*[move arms in front of body in "wiper" motion]*
swish, swish, swish	*[move arms in front of body in "wiper" motion]*
swish, swish, swish	*[move arms in front of body in "wiper" motion]*
The wipers on the bus go swish, swish, swish	*[move arms in front of body in "wiper" motion]*
All through the town	
★ ★ ★ ★ ★ ★	
The horn on the bus does beep, beep, beep	*[pretend to push horn]*
beep, beep, beep	*[pretend to push horn]*
beep, beep, beep	*[pretend to push horn]*
The horn on the bus does beep, beep, beep	*[pretend to push horn]*
All through the town	
★ ★ ★ ★ ★ ★	
The babies on the bus go waah, waah, waah	*[pretend to cry, i.e. rubbing eyes]*
waah, waah, waah	*[pretend to cry, i.e. rubbing eyes]*
waah, waah, waah	*[pretend to cry, i.e. rubbing eyes]*
The babies on the bus go waah, waah, waah	*[pretend to cry, i.e. rubbing eyes]*
All through the town	
★ ★ ★ ★ ★ ★	

The mommies on the bus go "shhh," "shhh," "shhh"	[put finger to your mouth and say "shhh," "shhh," "shhh"]
"shhh," "shhh," "shhh"	[put finger to your mouth and say "shhh," "shhh," "shhh"]
"shhh," "shhh," "shhh"	[put finger to your mouth and say "shhh," "shhh," "shhh"]
The mommies on the bus go "shhh," "shhh," "shhh"	[put finger to your mouth and say "shhh," "shhh," "shhh"]
All through the town	
★ ★ ★ ★ ★ ★	
The driver on the bus says "move on back"	[motion to the back of the bus with your thumb]
"move on back"	[motion to the back of the bus with your thumb]
"move on back"	[motion to the back of the bus with your thumb]
The driver on the bus says "move on back"	[motion to the back of the bus with your thumb]
All through the town	
★ ★ ★ ★ ★ ★	
The wheels on the bus go round and round	[roll arms in front of body]
round and round	[roll arms in front of body]
round and round	[roll arms in front of body]
The wheels on the bus go round and round	[roll arms in front of body]
All through the town	

HAND-CLAPPING SONGS AND GAMES

These build brains and social-emotional skills with four hands and two people.

Purpose

Hand-clapping songs help your child learn to work cooperatively with a partner to achieve a common goal—in this case, the goal of patting hands together in a pattern and sequence of movements while singing. Singing and rhythmically coordinating your hands with another person's hands is challenging and demands focus, concentration and eye contact. In addition, children learn to control their bodies; they learn not to slap but to pat hands gently. Hand–clapping songs also provide opportunities to develop physical skills of hand–eye coordination. (See more in Chapter 5.) Hand-clapping songs are perfect for a parent and child as well as two children on a playdate!

How to

Teach your child either by learning the song first and then adding the claps, or by singing slowly and teaching the movements at the same time.

- To teach the song first, try using the echo method: Sing each line, and then ask your child to "echo" you. Go through the entire song one line at a time. Then do the same thing, singing two lines each time, then three lines, and so on. Then teach the movements as you both sing together.

- To teach the song and movements at the same time, sit facing your child and ask her to mirror all of your movements while you sing. Slowly count to 4 and then sing and do all motions—but don't worry about the beat yet—just focus on helping your child learn the song and the motions. As you and your child outstretch your hands, gently make contact with each other's hands.

- Encourage your child to make eye contact with you, watch and copy your movements, and have fun! Remind him that making mistakes is how we learn and not to worry if he messes up (or if you do!). You can model making a mistake by doing a wrong movement and then correcting yourself. As he learns the song, slowly sing it to a steady beat. As he masters the song and the movements, increase the speed!

Below are two fun and easy hand-clapping songs to get started on.

"Pat-a-Cake"

Traditional

Pat-a-cake, pat-a-cake	[clap hands 1x and cross right hand to meet partner's right hand, clap hands 1x and cross left hand to meet partner's left hand]
baker's man	[repeat same movements as above]
Bake me a cake as	[repeat same movements as above]
fast as you can	[repeat same movements as above]
Pat it, roll it and mark it with a B	[pretend to pat, roll and write the letter "B" in your dough]
Put it in the oven for baby and me	[pretend to put your dough in the oven]
★ ★ ★ ★ ★ ★	
Pat-a-cake, pat-a-cake	[clap hands 1x and cross right hand to meet partner's right hand, clap hands 1x and cross left hand to meet partner's left hand]
baker's man	[repeat same movements as above]
Bake me a cake	[repeat same movements as above]
as fast as you can	[repeat same movements as above]
Roll it up, roll it up	[pretend to roll dough]
And throw it in a pan	[pretend to throw dough in a pan]
Pat-a-cake, pat-a-cake	[clap hands 1x and cross right hand to meet partner's right hand, clap hands 1x and cross left hand to meet partner's left hand]
baker's man	[repeat same movements as above]

"Miss Mary Mack"

Traditional

Miss Mary	[arms crossed with hands on chest, tap knees with hands, clap hands]
Mack	[cross right hand to meet partner's right hand and then clap own hands 1x]
Mack	[cross left hand to meet partner's left hand and then clap own hands 1x]
Mack	[cross right hand to meet partner's right hand and then clap own hands 1x]
All dressed in	[arms crossed with hands on chest, tap knees with hands, clap hands]

cont.

Black	[cross right hand to meet partner's right hand and then clap own hands 1x]
Black	[cross left hand to meet partner's left hand and then clap own hands 1x]
Black	[cross right hand to meet partner's right hand and then clap own hands 1x]
	[NOTE: repeat same pattern for rest of the song]
With silver buttons, buttons, buttons	
All down her back, back, back	
She asked her mother, mother, mother	
for fifty cents, cents, cents	
To see the elephants, elephants, elephants	
Jump the fence, fence, fence.	
They jumped so high, high, high	
they reached the sky, sky, sky	
And didn't come back, back, back	
'Til the fourth of July, July, July.	

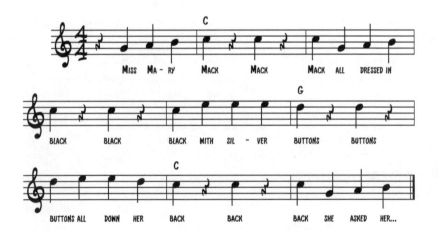

(CONTINUE SAME MELODY WITH THESE LYRICS)
MOTHER, MOTHER, MOTHER
FOR FIFTY CENTS, CENTS, CENTS
TO SEE THE ELEPHANTS, ELEPHANTS, ELEPHANTS
JUMP THE FENCE, FENCE, FENCE
THEY JUMPED SO HIGH, HIGH, HIGH
THEY REACHED THE SKY, SKY, SKY
AND THEY DIDN'T COME BACK, BACK, BACK
'TIL THE FOURTH OF JULY, JULY, JULY

 **Personal reflections**

I have fond memories of watching girls in my elementary school doing hand-clapping games. It was a great way for them to spend time, work together on intricately synchronized tasks and to show off! I did manage to learn a couple of super simple hand-clapping song patterns as a child!

What are your children's favorite hand-clapping songs?

Notes

PARTNER DANCES

Partner dances are great for learning to develop interactive skills. Your child will learn to coordinate movements with just one other person. Multiple partners can engage in partner dances at the same time.

"Brother, Sister, Dance with Me"

Adaptation from the opera Hansel and Gretel
by Engelbert Humperdinck (1881)

Purpose

"Brother, Sister, Dance with Me" helps your child learn to cooperate and maintain eye contact while coordinating movement sequences with his partner. In addition, he will practice controlling his body and following directions.

How to

Pair up each child so that he's facing a partner (which can be you!). For a group of children, you can have one line of children standing shoulder to shoulder facing their partners in another line of children, also standing shoulder to shoulder. You can also have the pairs dispersed randomly throughout the room. Follow the directions in the song.

Remind the children to move slowly, follow the directions and keep with the beat of the music. Remind children who don't get their "first choice" partner that they will have chances to dance with other partners in the future. You may want to sing the song several times and change partners each time, so that children get a chance to dance with a variety of partners.

Brother, sister, dance with me	[bow to partner]
Take both of my hands	[hold hands with partner]
Once this way, once that way	[partners step one way, then other way]
Round and round, it's not hard	[partners go in circle 1x in clockwise direction]
★ ★ ★ ★ ★ ★	
With your hands, you clap, clap, clap	[each person claps hands 3x]
With your feet, you tap, tap, tap	[each person alternates feet stomping on floor 3x]
Once this way, once that way	[partners step one way, then other way]
Round and round, it's not hard	[partners go in circle 1x in clockwise direction]
★ ★ ★ ★ ★ ★	
With your head, you nod, nod, nod	[nod head 3x]
With your fingers, you snap, snap, snap	[each person snaps fingers 3x or opens and closes fingers and thumb 3x]
Once this way, once that way	[partners step one way, then other way]
Round and round, it's not hard	[partners go in circle 1x in clockwise direction]
★ ★ ★ ★ ★ ★	
Oh, you did that really well	[bow to partner]
Oh, I wouldn't have guessed!	[shake partner's hand]
Once this way, once that way	[partners step one way, then other way]
Round and round, it's not hard	[partners go in circle 1x in clockwise direction]

D · A

BROT - HER SIS - TER DANCE WITH ME   TA - KE BOTH   OF   MY HANDS

D   G   A   D

ONCE THIS WAY   ONCE THAT WAY   ROUND AND ROUND   IT'S NOT HARD

"Nabe, Nabe, Soku Nuke"

Traditional

Purpose

In this Japanese partner dance "Nabe, Nabe, Soku Nuke," children learn to work with a partner in holding hands while inverting their bodies, increasing the number of times each round. They learn to coordinate movements and follow directions.

How to

I recommend demonstrating this song slowly with a partner before having them try it on their own with a peer—as the movements can be a little tricky. Pair up each child with a partner (which can be you!). Have them each face and hold their partner's hands. Halfway through the song direct them to invert their bodies while maintaining holding hands so that they are standing back to back. At the end of the song they invert their bodies while maintaining holding hands so they are back facing each other again. The second time through the song, direct them halfway through to invert their bodies in a complete revolution so they are facing each other. Do the same thing at the end of the song. You can then encourage them to invert their bodies 2x both halfway through and at the end of the song.

Note: If it is too challenging for your child to invert his body while holding hands, I have seen videos online of children and parents inverting their bodies while each holding alternate ends of a scarf or small towel.

Nabe, nabe,	*[face partner and hold hands]*
soku nuke.	*[invert bodies while maintaining hand holding so that you are back to back]*
Sokoganuketara.	*[stand back to back]*
Kaerimasho.	*[invert bodies while maintaining hand holding so that you are facing each other]*

NA - BE, NA - BE,   SO - KU NU-KE.   SO KO- GA NU- KE-TA-RA.   KA-E-RI-MA- SHO.

👍 Personal reflections

I have used partner dances individually when working with one child and in classrooms with large groups of children to help them both learn music and social skills. I find them to be great opportunities to learn to control one's body, to have fun and to learn to follow directions while having fun with a partner.

Which partner dance does your child like best?

Notes

CIRCLE DANCES

Circle dances and games provide a supportive structure for groups of children to participate together while working side-by-side and together. Rules learned in one song can be easily transferred to others, helping build confidence and increasing social competence.

"Ring Around the Rosie"

Traditional

Purpose

"Ring Around the Rosie" helps children learn to work together and follow directions while holding hands and moving in a circle. They will learn a basic structure within which they can apply other movements, e.g. "Jump Around the Rosie" or "Dance Around the Rosie."

How to

Direct your children (you can play "Ring Around the Rosie" with one child but it's also fun to play with a group of children on a playdate, at a party or at daycare or preschool) to make a circle holding hands, facing inwards. Sing the song while slowly moving in a clockwise direction. On the word "down" encourage everyone to let go of each other's hands and gently drop to the floor. Chant the second part of the song while standing up and re-forming your circle. Repeat until done.

Ring around the rosie	*[hold hands and circle to the left]*
Pocket full of posie	
Ashes, ashes	
We all fall down	*[gently fall down]*
★ ★ ★ ★ ★ ★	
Cows are in the meadow	*[slowly stand up and hold hands in circle]*
Eating buttercups	
Ashes, ashes	
We all stand up	

Variations

For the word "ring," try inserting "jump," "dance" or "tip toe," or another action verb of your choice.

 Personal reflections

I love to sing this song at my performances with The Bossy Frog Band. We added a funky pop music beat to the song which gives it a little more modern feel.

What variations to "Ring Around the Rosie" did you and your children come up with?

Notes

"Bluebird"

Traditional

Purpose

Children learn to take turns being the main character, or "bluebird," while the group learns to work together holding hands and letting the "bluebird" fly under their raised arms.

How to

For "Bluebird," I recommend having 3–6 children in total. Choose one child to be the "bluebird," who stands outside the circle. Have the rest of the children make a circle holding hands, facing inwards. As you and the children sing the song, have the "bluebird" fly through the "windows"— the raised arms of the children holding hands. (You may need to remind the children to raise their arms as the "bluebird" tries to fly through their window.) The "bluebird" should fly into and out of the circle throughout the song. Once the song ends, have the "bluebird" choose another child to be the "bluebird," and repeat until all children have had a turn.

Bluebird, bluebird through my window
Bluebird, bluebird through my window
Bluebird, bluebird through my window
Oh, Johnny I am tired

Take another child and tap them on the shoulder
Take another child and tap them on the shoulder
Take another child and tap them on the shoulder
Oh, Johnny I am tired

👍 Personal reflections

I also like to sing this song while teaching children how to play the triangle. They can put the striker inside the triangle, pretending the striker is the bluebird and the triangle is the window.

Which circle dances does your child like best?

Notes

FREEZE DANCES

From go/stop to red light/green light to freeze dances, children love the challenge of controlling their bodies on command.

Purpose

Freeze dances help children learn to participate in a group activity, but as individuals spaced around the room engaged in their own movements. They will learn to listen, control their bodies and focus their attention by stopping on command. They also provide good opportunities to practice respecting personal space by freely dancing near each other without touching.

How to

You can "Freeze Dance" with one child or a group of children. Choose a fun recording of a danceable song or a song that you can sing while playing a drum or tambourine. This can be a children's song or a child-appropriate pop song. Remind the children of the rules of the game, which include keeping good personal space, always being in control of one's body, and when the music plays, dancing, and when the music stops, "freezing."

Play the recording or sing the song. Randomly stop the recording or stop singing. You can also say "freeze" to reinforce and remind the children to stop.

In some freeze songs, anyone who doesn't freeze at the end of the song must sit out the rest of the game. For young children aged five and under, I *do not* include this "you're out" aspect. Instead, if a child moves after the music stops, I just remind everyone to freeze and praise all those who are doing their best to try to stop. The competitive aspect of the "you're out" rule is difficult for young children to manage and is better for older children.

Variations

- Give one of the children the responsibility of the "freeze" job.

- Encourage children to dance in different ways before freezing—for example, with both arms up in the air, or while hopping on one foot.

- Give the children scarves or pom poms to use while dancing.

Personal reflections

I have found freeze dances to be incredibly engaging with groups of children of all abilities, skills and challenges. Never underestimate the power of the "freeze"!

Which recorded songs are your child's favorite to freeze dance to?

Notes

PASSING GAME SONGS

Passing game songs are amazing opportunities to build important social skills.

"Obwisana"

Traditional

Purpose

"Obwisana" is a passing game song from Ghana. Children learn to take turns and follow directions, to work together as a group to keep the pattern and pace going at the same rhythm of the song. They learn to adjust their passing to the speed of the song.

How to

While I have simplified this song for young children, I recommend it for children four years old and older due to the complexity of having to pass an object in tempo. Have children sit in a circle facing inward. You can play "Obwisana" with two people, but it's a great song to do with three to six. Start by singing the song and tapping your knees on the beat to show them the speed that they will be passing the object. Encourage them to sing and tap along with you, keeping the same steady beat. Next, sing and pass a pretend object on the words "sana" and "sa." Tap in front of each child for when they would receive and then pass the object. Encourage them to pretend pass with you. When they understand the basic concept, add a real object to pass (e.g. rhythm shaker egg, bean bag, potato or any small object that is easy to hold and pass). As you sing the song, direct the children by pointing to them when it's their turn to pass the one object. Have them pass it in a clockwise direction on the words "sana" and "sa."

Obwisana sana	[on the word "sana" place object in front of person to your left]
Obwisana sa	[on the word "sa" place object in front of person to your left]
Obwisana sana	[on the word "sana" place object in front of person to your left]
Obwisana sa	[on the word "sa" place object in front of person to your left]

Variations

After the children have successfully mastered passing one object, stop the song and give the group a second object. Have them try to pass the objects simultaneously. When they can successfully pass two objects, add a third. Keep adding until everyone is passing and receiving an object at the same time.

"Bounce High"

Traditional

Purpose

"Bounce High" helps children learn to work with a partner (you or a friend) or group while keeping a steady beat and chanting. They learn to control their bodies, make eye contact, follow directions and engage in a task together. They are also developing the physical skills of balance and hand–eye coordination. This is a great song to help a child who has particular challenges with sharing, taking turns or waiting for their turn. I have played this song with just one other child as well as in groups of 12 children.

How to

Demonstrate how to bounce a ball on the floor and catch it while rhythmically chanting "bounce, catch, bounce, catch" repeatedly with a steady beat. Then demonstrate the same bouncing/catching pattern while chanting the lyrics to "Bounce High." Bounce the ball on the word "bounce" and catch on the word "high." Bounce again on "bounce the" and catch on "ball to." Continue this pattern throughout the song. Then have your child stand facing you, about four feet away. This time, chant the song and bounce the ball to them on the word "bounce" and have them catch on "high." Have them bounce to you on "bounce" and catch on the word "low." Continue with chanting and bouncing and catching to a steady beat.

See variations below for ways to use this song with a group of children.

Bounce high	[bounce the ball to partner on the word "bounce"]
Bounce low	[partner bounces to you on the word "bounce"]
Bounce the ball to	[bounce the ball to partner on the word "bounce"]
Shiloh	[partner bounces to you on the word "bounce"]

Variations

- Try this with a group of three to six children standing in a circle. Have each child bounce the ball to the person on his or her left, all the while chanting and keeping the beat. When the group has mastered bouncing one ball, add a second, and then a third, until every child has a ball and is simultaneously bouncing and catching!

- You can also try this with a group using one ball, but the "bouncer" can bounce to anyone in the circle when it's time to chant "Shiloh." Instead of chanting "Shiloh," however, the bouncer should substitute the name of the person to whom she or he is bouncing the ball.

(For example, "Bounce high, bounce low, bounce the ball to... Jeremy.") Sing the song again and have Jeremy chant the name of and bounce the ball to a new person instead of "Shiloh."

👍 Personal reflections

While I have found this to be a highly stimulating and fun social experience for many children I work with, I have also found that some children kick or throw the ball—something they are more used to doing when playing with balls outside. They may need reminders that there is no throwing or kicking the balls during this activity. It's important to remind children to always be in control when bouncing balls during music games.

I recommend the "bouncing" version for children aged four to five years old, as bouncing and catching can be challenging for younger children. For two- to three-year-olds, you can try sitting on the floor and rolling, rather than bouncing, the ball.

How was your "Bounce High" experience?

Notes

ECHO SONGS

While not traditionally considered "play" songs, I snuck echo songs in here as they give children opportunities to learn to lead and follow and have instant social success. They are also great for building language skills.

Purpose

The echo song "No More Pie" gives children an opportunity for instant musical success through echoing when they are a responder and gratification from leading when they are the caller. Echo songs can help children develop skills to lead others by making eye contact and communicating in a clear and assertive way to get the group to echo them. Children can develop an appreciation for working together as a group and for how listening and following directions can lead to beautiful music. Echo songs are also great to work on speech and language skills as children can improve their speech fluency through trying to echo short phrases and keeping the same beat as the leader.

How to

Sing the first line of the song and point to yourself. Immediately after, point to the group and mouth the words you just sang, encouraging them to echo you. Do this for each line of the song. After you have sung the song several times through, ask for volunteers to try leading.

"No More Pie"

Traditional

Note: The leader sings the part in the left column and the "echoer" imitates with the part in the right column.

Leader: Oh, my	*Echoer:* Oh, my
No more pie!	No more pie!
Pie's too sweet	Pie's too sweet
I want a piece of meat.	I want a piece of meat.
★ ★ ★ ★ ★ ★	
Meat's too red,	Meat's too red,
I want a piece of bread.	I want a piece of bread.
Bread's too brown,	Bread's too brown,
Go to town.	Go to town.
★ ★ ★ ★ ★ ★	
Town's too far,	Town's too far,
Take a car.	Take a car.
Car's too slow,	Car's too slow,
I fell and stubbed my toe.	I fell and stubbed my toe.
★ ★ ★ ★ ★ ★	
Toe gives me pain,	Toe gives me pain,
Take a train.	Take a train.

cont.

Train had a wreck,	Train had a wreck,
I hurt my neck.	I hurt my neck.
★ ★ ★ ★ ★ ★	
Oh, my!	Oh, my!
No more pie.	No more pie.

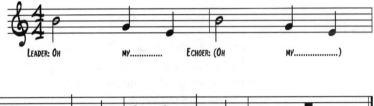

NOTE: CONTINUE EACH LINE OF SONG USING THIS MELODY

👍 Personal reflections

"No More Pie" happens to be one of my favorite songs to use when working with young children. I find echo songs in general to be wonderful opportunities for children to have successful musical experiences, whether with one other person or in large groups.

How was your "Echo Song" experience?

Notes

MOVEMENT PLAY SONGS

We'll explore movement play songs more deeply in Chapter 5, but I included "If You're Happy and You Know It" here as it's also a great song to learn about expressing different feelings.

"If You're Happy and You Know It"

Traditional

Purpose

Movement play songs such as "If You're Happy and You Know It" help children learn to listen, follow directions and work together side-by-side, engaging in the same motions and singing. You can also adapt this song to help children learn about different feelings and different ways to express them.

How to

Sing the traditional version with accompanying fill-in words and movements. Talk about things that make you happy and ask the children to talk about the ways they express happiness.

If you're happy and you know it clap your hands	[clap, clap]
If you're happy and you know it clap your hands	[clap, clap]
If you're happy and you know it and you really want to show it	
If you're happy and you know it clap your hands	[clap, clap]
★ ★ ★ ★ ★ ★	
If you're happy and you know it stomp your feet	[stomp, stomp]
If you're happy and you know it stomp your feet	[stomp, stomp]
If you're happy and you know it and you really want to show it	
If you're happy and you know it stomp your feet	[stomp, stomp]
★ ★ ★ ★ ★ ★	
If you're happy and you know it shout hooray	["hooray!"]
If you're happy and you know it shout hooray	["hooray!"]
If you're happy and you know it and you really want to show it	
If you're happy and you know it shout hooray	["hooray!"]

Variations

Ask your child for suggestions of movements to represent happiness—for example, "If you're happy and you know it, ride a bike!" Model the action that should accompany the new movement—or let the children create it for themselves. You can also explore ways to express other feelings such as "If You're Sad and You Know It" or "If You're Mad and You Know It." Ask children to come up with different actions for the feelings chosen.

👍 Personal reflections

This is another song that children universally love and easily learn. I like to do a lot of variations on this song, especially coming up with new silly movements for different feelings.

What variations did you and your child come up with?

Notes

INSTRUMENT SONGS AND GAMES

Get out the tambourines, maracas and drums and start a band! Instruments are wonderful for building social-emotional skills and for great playdates.

Purpose

Musical instruments offer children opportunities to interact socially and express themselves without words. They are fun, shiny, magical objects that make many different interesting sounds and convey many different feelings. They can help children build social-emotional skills through learning how to listen, lead, take turns and share.

How to

Break out a basket of instruments. Try a variety of unstructured and structured musical activities as described below.

- **Unstructured rhythm band:** My recommendation is to provide some basic limits on volume and sharing and then letting your child or children experiment with sound play. You may want to check in on them periodically to make sure there is adequate sharing and turn taking so that everyone is happy.

- **Structured rhythm band:** Try singing a simple song, such as "When the Saints Go Marching In," and encouraging your child to play along. Try to resist giving too many instructions as this may dampen their fun and curiosity. You can also sing a word or phrase and ask your child or children to echo you on their instruments.

"When the Saints Go Marching In"

Traditional

Oh, when the saints go marching in
Oh, when the saints go marching in
Oh Lord I want to be in that number
When the saints go marching in

Oh, when the cymbals go "crash, crash, crash"
Oh, when the cymbals go "crash, crash, crash"
Oh Lord I want to be in that number
When the cymbals go "crash, crash, crash"

Note: Try inserting any instrument into the above verse to highlight the instruments that your marching band is playing.

- **Parade:** Many children enjoy a parade. Distribute hand-held instruments, i.e. maracas, tambourines, bells and small drums, to your child or children and march around the room single file. You can assign a leader of the parade for the rest of the musicians to follow. After a minute of marching, ask the leader to go to the back of the line and have the next in line be the leader. Encourage the musicians to stay in line and close to the person in front of them. Try singing a song to give them some rhythmic structure for their marching. You can try varying the tempo of your singing and instruct them to march fast when you sing fast and slowly when you sing slowly.

"I Don't Care if the Rain Comes Down" (using rainsticks)

Traditional

Purpose

Rainsticks offer children the opportunity to learn to wait—children turn the rainstick over and have to wait until all the beads have fallen and the sound stops before they turn it back again. Playing with rainsticks can also help them learn to focus and listen closely (they need to pay attention to the sounds from the stick), and to share (they can pass the stick to a friend when their turn is over). Using the rainstick with "I Don't Care if the Rain Comes Down" provides both simple fun and imaginative play, as they pretend that the rainstick sounds are raindrops.

How to

Preface your rainstick play with talking about how waiting can be difficult to do but can often be a good thing. When we wait, we can learn new ways to do the activity from watching others. It also allows for everyone to get a turn. Tell them that there's a musical instrument that only plays when you wait. Get out your rainstick and demonstrate how to use it by turning it over and waiting until all of the sound stops before turning it back. Ask the children what it sounds like. After a few guesses, tell them it's called a rainstick because many people think it sounds like rain.

Turn it over again and ask them to wait with you and nicely say the word "turn" when all the sound finishes. Have each child turn the stick over three times and wait for the sound to stop before passing it to the next child. While each child takes a turn with the rainstick, sing "I Don't Care if the Rain Comes Down." Make sure every child has a turn.

I don't care if the rain comes down
I'm gonna dance all day
I don't care if the rain comes down
I'm gonna dance all day

Hey, hey carry me away
I'm gonna dance all day
Hey, hey carry me away
I'm gonna dance all day

Variations

If you and your child are playing with the rainstick—as opposed to playing in a group—hand the stick back and forth between you after three turns each.

👍 Personal reflections

For many children, musical instruments are magical objects. They look at them in awe as if they possess some mystical power. In some sense they do, as they are able to convey and change deep intimate feelings. My recommendation is to not underestimate the power of musical instruments to engage and educate young children.

What musical instruments do your children like using?

What creative ways do they play with them?

Notes

4

SLEEP THROUGH MUSIC

Using Music for Better Bedtimes and More Restful Night Times

Children need sleep. Parents need sleep. Families are happier and healthier when everyone is well rested. Let's face it, we all need sleep! Sleep is good for us. Sleep matters.

Sleep is increasingly being recognized as a major factor in overall health and wellbeing. Many experts feel it is as important to a child's development as love and nutrition. In the words of pediatrician Ronald Dahl (2007) (and the capital letters are his, not mine):

> BROADLY SPEAKING, IT MIGHT BE ARGUED THAT THE MOST FUNDAMENTAL REQUIREMENTS FOR HEALTHY GROWTH AND DEVELOPMENT IN YOUNG CHILDREN include a) loving support and protection by parents/caretakers, b) adequate nutrition, and c) adequate sleep. (p.1079)

Sleep affects much more than just the amount of energy children have during the day. When children get the appropriate quantity and quality of sleep, a lot of good things happen. For young children, sleep is a restorative process: during sleep bodies grow, brains develop, and learning is solidified in memory (Adam 1980; Tham, Schneider and Broekman 2017).

RESEARCH SHOWS

In the early years, sleep helps with language development (Dionne *et al.* 2011), and children who get an age-appropriate amount of sleep are more optimistic and have higher self-esteem (Lemola *et al.* 2011). Getting too little sleep has more repercussions than just being tired and cranky; it impacts most areas of learning and development as well as physical health. Too little sleep in early childhood can lead to problems with obesity, diabetes and heart disease later in life (Bathory and Tomopoulos 2017). Lack of sleep can lead to symptoms that mimic ADHD (Schuster 2018).

And sleep not only impacts individual development. It affects the entire family. Tired parents have "less gas in the tank" to be there for their children. When there are sleep disruptions, an entire family or classroom can be sunk! Well-rested parents are parents with more to offer their child. A rested parent has access to more internal resources to support responsive parenting and can connect in a more loving, patient and compassionate manner.

Sleep problems

Childhood difficulty with sleep is more common than you may think. Some 20 to 30 percent of children have sleep problems (Mindell *et al.* 2006). That's a lot of tired children!

The most common sleep problems are referred to as "bedtime resistance" and "night wakings."

- Bedtime resistance is what you imagine—refusing to go to sleep at bedtime, getting out of bed and crying, calling persistently for a parent.

- Night wakings are when a child has difficulty falling back to sleep after waking up at night in between sleep cycles.

There is a variety of factors that contribute to sleep problems. If your child has trouble falling asleep or wakes frequently in the night, you may want to explore the various factors that impact that behavior, including your child's individual temperament, what's happening for her developmentally or educationally at the moment, and any associations he may have developed around falling asleep and bedtime. Some sleep problems are due to other potentially more serious conditions and respond to different interventions. It is recommended to consult your pediatrician or other sleep professional in these circumstances.

Children's temperaments vary

Some children are more sensitive to their environment. Light, noise or the emotional atmosphere in their environment may be overly stimulating. This may impact their ability to calm themselves and go to sleep.

Children respond as they develop new abilities

For some children, the development of new abilities can contribute to keeping them up at night. For example, as children develop "object permanence," commonly thought to begin in the middle of the first year, they begin to understand that objects and people continue to exist even when they can't be seen or heard anymore. This new understanding may be accompanied by fears such as "separation anxiety"—a fear that someone or something now out of view will not return. Due to their expanding imaginations, some children may imagine scary things— monsters under the bed or in the closet—and these fears often arise at bedtime or during the night, causing sleep problems.

It's not always fears that keep them up. Acquiring new skills, like sitting up or standing, can contribute to sleep problems; children are sometimes so excited that they practice them as much as they can, including at bedtime or in the middle of the night when they wake up. My children were so excited by their new-found physical skills that they practiced climbing out of their cribs at bedtime. As exciting as this was for them, it was not conducive for their, or my, getting a good night's rest!

Children link objects—and people—to sleep

Many children also develop associations to things that they link with sleep. As you might imagine, this might be a special stuffed animal or a blanket that they need in order to soothe themselves to fall asleep. But this can also be us! When our children are resisting bedtime and we consistently stay with them to soothe them to sleep, our behavior can actually reinforce their own resistant behavior—they learn to associate us with sleep, and they therefore need us in order to fall asleep (Morgenthaler *et al.* 2006).

Sleep hygiene

There are things we can all do to improve our child's sleep. These strategies—labeled "sleep hygiene" by the National Foundation of Sleep—can improve both the quality and the quantity of sleep for the whole family.

While different families and cultures have a wide variety of ways and timelines to achieve this, the goal of helping our children practice good sleep hygiene is for them to learn to independently soothe themselves and fall asleep. These are important skills to learn, especially in infancy. They are skills that children can use throughout their lives, that contribute to healthy development and physical health, both in the short and long term, and that can lead to happier families!

While each child is unique and needs different quantities of sleep depending on their temperament, developmental stage, individual needs and cultural expectations, there are general guidelines for the average amount of sleep children should get every day by age. The National Foundation of Sleep (Hirshkowitz *et al.* 2015) suggests the following quantities:

- 14–17 hours of sleep for the first three months

- 12–15 hours for babies aged 4–11 months

- 11–14 hours for one- to two-year-olds

- 10–13 hours for preschoolers, aged three to five years old.

The ABCs of Sleeping

A 2016 study by Allen and colleagues reviewed evidence-based research to find common practices that worked for developing good sleep hygiene in the early years. As a result, the researchers came up with a mnemonic, the ABCs of Sleeping.

Age-appropriate Bedtimes and wake-times with Consistency	Age-appropriate bedtimes depend on when a child needs to wake up in order to get the right amount of sleep. Count the hours backwards from when the child needs to wake up to make sure he is getting enough hours. But don't ignore signs of drowsiness; if your child seems sleepy, let him go to bed!
Schedules and routines	Schedules and routines are helpful in almost every aspect of parenting and can be especially so at bedtime. Bedtime routines should become progressively calmer as "lights off" time approaches and may include activities like brushing teeth, bathing, reading books and singing songs.
Location	Beds are for sleeping, and sleeping is for beds. Don't make children's beds play areas—no dance parties on the bed!—and don't expect them to sleep on the couch or on the floor.
Exercise and diet	An appropriate amount of vigorous exercise and a well-balanced, nutritional diet throughout the day will contribute to a good night's sleep.
Electronics banned from the bedroom and at bedtime	This is a tough one in today's electronic-driven world. But handing your child a tablet or cell phone to calm her before bed is actually working at cross-purposes, many researchers have found. Video stimulation is intense and will interfere with a child's ability to wind down. It will also complicate her ability to learn to calm herself before sleep, since she may become dependent on this tool.
Positivity	How we as parents feel about sleep and bedtime can affect our child's attitudes about going to sleep. If we are positive and relaxed, our child is likely to be, too; if we show stress or anger, our child may have more difficulty going to sleep.
Independence when falling asleep	Ideally, children should learn to fall asleep independently in their own beds without us in the room. Complete any parts of the bedtime routine that take place elsewhere (like brushing teeth), and then put the child to bed. This will encourage them to self-soothe and to learn to put themselves back to sleep independently if they wake during the night.
Needs of child met during the day	When their needs are met consistently and responsively throughout the day, children are more likely to approach bedtime in a more relaxed and calm mood and be more able to soothe themselves during night wakings.
equal Great sleep	Practicing good sleep hygiene will not only help your child accept and enjoy the arrival of bedtime, but it will mean a better night's sleep for you as a parent!

Music and sleep hygiene

Music can play a big role both in helping your child learn strategies for "good sleep hygiene" and in your having a well-rested family. It's no coincidence that lullabies are one of the most common types of songs for young children. Music can help children calm down and relax, is easily associated with bedtimes, can be a part of bedtime routines, and can help children learn to independently soothe themselves to sleep. And music is a powerful way to meet your children's needs during the day in a responsive and loving way, so they are more "ready for bed" and able to soothe themselves during the night.

Music can play a part in virtually all the "ABCs" of sleep. Some of these strategies will work for your individual child and some won't. Try them all, and when you find what works, do it consistently!

Age-appropriate music at age-appropriate bedtimes

As you establish consistent, age-appropriate bedtimes and wake-times, use music that is age-appropriate as part of your bedtime routine. Pick simple children's lullabies that use music that young brains can easily perceive and process. Lullabies are slow, gentle songs with calming themes. Children will tune out from music that is too cognitively complicated; they will get over-stimulated by music that is too fast and/or loud. The small-note steps, slow tempo, repetition and childish themes in most lullabies will more likely interest and engage your children without over-stimulating them.

Start your bedtime routine with a musical transition

As your child's bedtime rolls around, signal that it's time for the routine to begin by playing or singing a calming "bedtime transition" song. Find one or two songs for this purpose that you consistently play when it's time to start winding down. Your child will begin to subconsciously associate those songs with bedtime and help her begin to calm herself.

Include your child in developing their sleep routines by asking her to pick some of the songs to play. This can be fun and help her be more invested in the process. This can also help her learn how to make and follow through on a plan and complete a task. If she picks songs that are too stimulating, try offering your child two or three calm songs to choose from, and let her pick one or two to listen to or sing every night. Your child will feel control over the process—but within the limits you set.

If at first your child doesn't appear to respond to the relaxing music, have patience, and try waiting a few more minutes.

One of the best things about including music in your bedtime routine is that you can take it anywhere. You can sing and listen to your songs and music at bedtime at home, on vacation, when visiting grandma and grandpa—or give a list (or even a recording) of your children's favorite lullabies to their daycare provider or preschool teacher.

Unfortunately, beds are not for dancing

Don't make the bed your dance party area. Remember, beds are for sleeping. We want our children to associate their beds with sleep, not a rock concert. The dance party is probably better off outside the bedroom and before dinner, or right afterwards, with enough quiet time afterwards to help calm down and relax.

Rock out...during the day

Remember that dance party? Make sure you do have a solid dance party—or some other physical activity—during the day. Children need exercise for many reasons, not the least of which is to make bedtime easier for everyone.

Be in the musical moment...not with the music video

There is almost universal agreement among child development experts that allowing children to play electronic games or watch videos on phones, tablets, computers or TV at bedtime will negatively impact their ability to go to sleep. Video screens over-stimulate. Listen to music at bedtime without a video or screen of any kind. Videos and screens keep young brains jumping around when they should be calming down; they impact children's ability to independently soothe themselves; and they detract from the important intimacy that you and your child can share when engaging in a musical experience together.

Music for calming, relaxing and positive bedtimes

Enjoying music together can lead to a more positive attitude towards sleep and a more relaxing atmosphere around bedtime. (There is a biological basis for this: As we mentioned in Chapter 3, singing together actually makes our bodies release oxytocin, which helps us feel more socially connected and happier and decreases levels of the stress hormone cortisol (Kreutz 2014).) Music can also help children slow down their body rhythms as they slow down their bodies and heart rates and join with the calm, slow rhythms of lullabies. And when we sing lovingly and calmly, we are also helping them join with our positive and relaxed mood and attitude towards sleep and bedtime.

Singing and listening to music can also help a child let go of stimulating thoughts racing through their heads. The early years are an exciting time with new skills, experiences, activities and fears developing every day. Helping children listen to the words and slow gliding melodies and feeling the slow pulse of the rhythm of lullabies can help them learn to let go of all of the stimulation, excitement and anxiety, and to move into a more relaxed state.

Lullaby 'til drowsy only

Sing to help your children feel drowsy, but put them in bed before they fall asleep. While different families and cultures have different approaches and ages for this, good sleep hygiene helps children learn to soothe themselves in order for them to independently fall asleep... on their own. Remember the old adage, "You can give a man a fish and he'll eat for a day, but if you teach him to fish, he'll eat for a lifetime!" The same goes for sleep. "You can sing a lullaby until your child falls asleep, and they'll sleep for a night. But if you teach them how to soothe themselves independently, they'll fall asleep on their own for a lifetime. And feel good about their skills!"

Music for love and connection

Making music together can help children feel loved and connected to you and to feel good about themselves. A day with much "musical parenting" during the most simple everyday moments can help them go to bed with a smile on their faces and feeling as relaxed and calm as possible.

Having specific lullabies that your child associates with you and your shared relationship will help remind him that he is loved, lovable and capable of loving others. When children sing these songs at bed time, both when they're with you and when they are alone and trying to independently fall asleep, they will feel more comforted and confident.

Putting it all together

Music can help children develop good sleep hygiene. We can use music during the day to make sure that children get enough exercise so that they are tired at night, to help them calm themselves at bedtime, to feel loved and secure, to develop a positive association with bedtime and to eventually learn to independently fall asleep at night. It's no coincidence that lullabies are one of the most common types of children's song.

SONGS, GAMES AND ACTIVITIES FOR SLEEP

This section includes specific songs and musical activities that you can use to support your child in developing good sleep hygiene. The accompanying music and video files can be downloaded from www.jkp.com/voucher using the code BOOMESE.

ROCKING FOR DROWSINESS

Purpose

Holding and gently rocking your child to a steady beat while singing a lullaby is a great way to bond, calming to both body and mind. Children will join your slower beat eventually as you help them relax. Children benefit from physical contact to help them feel connected and to regulate their bodies, minds and feelings.

How to

Hold your child close to your body while singing a slow song and gently rocking to the beat. Have a set of two or three songs that you use for this purpose, so your child becomes familiar with them. You can also try matching the speed of your rocking to the rhythm of their breathing and gently slow down until they are more calm and relaxed.

Personal reflections

Some of my most cherished moments of the early years with my children are of holding them and rocking them to a steady beat to help them calm themselves. There was something intimate and special about being in rhythm with them until they could "let go" and relax.

What are your favorite memories of holding and rocking your child?

Notes

LULLABIES

Purpose

Lullabies help children calm their bodies, minds and feelings as they get ready to go to sleep. The slow pace and relaxing themes matched with your singing in a calm and gentle voice help them move towards drowsiness. The goal is not to sing them to sleep; rather, lullabies can help your children *transition towards* sleep. Lullabies can help them understand that it's time to get ready for bed as part of their nighttime routine, and also help them become drowsy as they get ready to independently fall asleep.

How to

Have a set of favorite lullabies for your child to choose from. Don't be afraid to add a new one to the set once in a while. You can sing the lullabies both to start your bedtime routine and once your child is in bed. I recommend having a set amount of songs you sing each night—perhaps two or three brief lullabies. If you don't, you may find yourself negotiating each night for how many and how long to sing.

Personal reflections

At my Bossy Frog Band concerts, I always include a lullaby in the middle of the show to help the children rest and rejuvenate before more dancing. I love singing the traditional lullaby from Puerto Rico, "Coqui." I have consistently found that many children will continue to dance and move during the first half of the song, but if I am patient and maintain a calm-sounding voice and slow tempo while singing, by the time I sing the second chorus, most if not all of the children are lying on the floor and resting calmly.

Which lullabies does your child like best?

Notes

"Hush Little Baby"

Traditional

Hush, little baby, don't say a word,
Mama's gonna buy you a mockingbird.

And if that mockingbird don't sing,
Mama's gonna buy you a diamond ring.

And if that diamond ring turns brass,
Mama's gonna buy you a looking glass.

And if that looking glass gets broke,
Mama's gonna buy you a billy goat.

And if that billy goat don't pull,
Mama's gonna buy you a cart and bull.

And if that cart and bull turn over
Mama's gonna buy you a dog named Rover.

And if that dog named Rover don't bark,
Mama's gonna buy you a horse and cart.

And if that horse and cart fall down,
You'll still be the sweetest little baby in town.

HUSH LIT-TLE BA - BY   DON'T SAY A WORD   MA- MA'S GON-NA BUY   YOU A

MOCK - ING   BIRD   AND   IF   THAT   MOCK - ING   BIRD   DON'T   SING

MA - MA'S   GON - NA   BUY   YOU   A   DIA - MOND   RING

(CONTINUE WITH THESE LYRICS)
AND IF THAT DIAMOND RING TURNS BRASS
MAMA'S GONNA BUY YOU A LOOKING GLASS
AND IF THAT LOOKING GLASS GETS BROKE
MAMA'S GONNA BUY YOU A BILLY GOAT
AND IF THAT BILLY GOAT DON'T PULL
MAMA'S GONNA BUY YOU A CART AND BULL
AND IF THAT CART AND BULL TURN OVER
MAMA'S GONNA BUY YOU A DOG NAMED ROVER
AND IF THAT DOG NAMED ROVER DON'T BARK
MAMA'S GONNA BUY YOU A HORSE AND CART
AND IF THAT HORSE AND CART FALL DOWN
YOU'LL STILL BE THE SWEETEST LITTLE BABY IN TOWN

"Frère Jacques"

Traditional

Frère Jacques, Frère Jacques,
Dormez-vous? Dormez-vous?
Sonnez les matines! Sonnez les matines!
Ding, dang, dong. Ding, dang, dong.

Are you sleeping? Are you sleeping?
Brother John, Brother John,
Morning bells are ringing! Morning bells are ringing!
Ding, dang, dong. Ding, dang, dong.

"Little Boy Blue"

Traditional

Little Boy Blue, come blow your horn,
The sheep's in the meadow, the cow's in the corn.
But where is the boy, who looks after the sheep?
He's under a haystack, fast asleep.
Will you wake him? No, not I,
For if I do, he's sure to cry.

"The Owl Song"

by Jeffrey Friedberg © 2008

Late at night sitting in a tree
The owl family sings to me
Hoo hoo hoo hoo hoo hoo hoo

Sleep all day and up all night
The owl family is quite a sight
Hoo hoo hoo hoo hoo hoo hoo

Hoo hoo hoo hoo hoo hoo
Hoo hoo hoo hoo hoo hoo hoo

The moon is up and the sun is down
The owl family makes quite a sound
Hoo hoo hoo hoo hoo hoo hoo

Mama and papa owl, baby owl too
On their branch they sing their tune
Hoo hoo hoo hoo hoo hoo hoo

Hoo hoo hoo hoo hoo hoo
Hoo hoo hoo hoo hoo hoo hoo

"Goodnight Little One"

by Jeffrey Friedberg © 2004

Goodnight little one
Goodnight little one
It's time to go to sleep
The sun is falling
And sleep is calling
And I love you

Close your tired eyes
Dream about butterflies
It's time to go to sleep
The sun is falling
And sleep is calling
And I love you

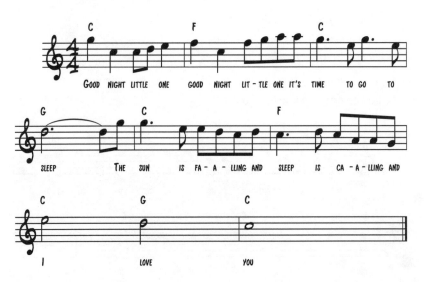

"Rocket Ship"

by Jeffrey Friedberg © 2004

Rocket ship take me to the sleepy place
In outer space, the sleepy place
Rocket ship take me to the sleepy place
In outer space, the sleepy place
We're gonna take a trip to places near and far
Up to the planets and around the stars
Put your head on your pillow close your tired eyes
Put your head on your pillow as we're gonna fly away

Close your eyes and think about the day to come
The rising sun, we'll all have fun
Close your eyes and think about the day to come
The rising sun, we'll all have fun
We're gonna take a trip to places near and far
Up to the planets and around the stars
Put your head on your pillow close your tired eyes
Put your head on your pillow as we're gonna fly away

Rocket ship is helping me to sleep tonight
So say goodnight, go to sleep tonight
Rocket ship is helping me to sleep tonight
So say goodnight, go to sleep tonight
We're gonna take a trip to places near and far
Up to the planets and around the stars
Put your head on your pillow close your tired eyes
Put your head on your pillow as we're gonna fly away

"NON-LULLABY" LULLABIES

The following songs are not typically thought of as lullabies, but their themes—love, peace, reunion with a loved one—and their gentle melodies and repetitive lyrics make them perfect potential sleep-inducers! I often sang "Little Wheel" to my children at bedtime, and it worked wonderfully. The promise in "My Bonnie" that the lovers will be reunited serves as a lovely, reassuring metaphor for what will happen in the morning, when your child wakes up and sees you once again.

"Little Wheel Turning in My Heart"

Traditional

There's a little wheel turning in my heart
There's a little wheel turning in my heart
In my heart, in my heart
There's a little wheel turning in my heart

There's a little song a singing in my heart
There's a little song a singing in my heart
In my heart, in my heart
There's a little song a singing in my heart

There's a little bell ringing in my heart
There's a little bell ringing in my heart
In my heart, in my heart
There's a little bell ringing in my heart

I feel so very happy in my heart
I feel so very happy in my heart
In my heart, in my heart
I feel so very happy in my heart

"Peace Like a River"

Traditional

I've got peace like a river
I've got peace like a river
I've got peace like a river
In my soul
I've got peace like a river
I've got peace like a river
I've got peace like a river
In my soul

I've got love like an ocean
I've got love like an ocean
I've got love like an ocean
In my soul
I've got love like an ocean
I've got love like an ocean
I've got love like an ocean
In my soul

I've got joy like a fountain
I've got joy like a fountain
I've got joy like a fountain
In my soul
I've got joy like a fountain
I've got joy like a fountain
I've got joy like a fountain
In my soul

"My Bonnie Lies Over the Ocean"

Traditional

My Bonnie lies over the ocean,
My Bonnie lies over the sea,
My Bonnie lies over the ocean,
Oh, bring back my Bonnie to me.

Bring back, bring back,
bring back my Bonnie to me, to me.
Bring back, bring back,
Oh, bring back my Bonnie to me.

5

PHYSICAL FITNESS AND MOTOR DEVELOPMENT THROUGH MUSIC

Building Healthier, Stronger and Better Coordinated Bodies with More Stamina!

Young children are movers. They move often and for many reasons. We want them to move a lot. Moving is good for them. Movement matters.

Even before they're born, children are kicking, elbowing and seemingly dancing in the womb. I remember feeling many strong kicks and elbows jutting out of my wife's belly when she was pregnant. Sometimes it seemed to be in response to the music we were listening to. I remember with our first child, when my wife was in her last trimester, we went to see the show *STOMP*, which was filled with incredibly active drumming and dancing on garbage can lids and other found objects. Throughout the show her belly was bouncing up and down. It was as if our child was dancing along to the music!

Movement and physical activity in the early years help children's bodies grow and develop through building strength, stamina, balance and coordination. Physical activity also helps children develop their body awareness as they learn to identify, label and control different parts of their bodies.

While the pace of physical development is unique to each child, the order and sequence is typically the same. And motor skill development is cumulative; each new skill builds on previously learned skills. Using "tummy time" to encourage children to lift their heads, for example, builds the strength, coordination and stamina to roll over, which in turn builds the abilities needed to sit up. And sitting up builds the strength, skills and abilities needed to stand, then to walk, then to run—and so on. Movement in the early years helps children build the physical skills and abilities they need in order to eventually manage their own needs independently. Some children, of course, will never be able to manage all their needs independently because of illness, an accident, or genetic or environmental constraints. The goal of physical development for every child should be to find ways for that child to be as independent as possible within his or her individual limits, through skill-building and with the help of adaptive technologies.

Physical activity affects all areas of development

Movement during the early years, however, is about more than just the development of a child's physical body. Physical activity and movement are part of a dynamic system. All domains of development are impacted simultaneously when children move. When they engage in physical activity, they are developing not only their motor skills but also their sense of self, and their cognitive, language, communication and social-emotional skills.

Children move for many different reasons, including:

- in order to gather sensory information and learn how things work

- to get things they want

- to get closer to—or farther away from—people or things

- to express and regulate feelings

- to exercise their growing feelings of independence and power

- to practice skills and to learn new skills

- to expel excess energy.

Physical activity helps children sleep better. Movement and physical activities help children have healthier bodies. Movement helps children better manage stress, anger, anxiety and depression. A moving child is a happier child. Children and families benefit when a child is physically active on a daily basis. As adults in their lives, we should provide as many opportunities as possible for children to involve and engage in all areas of development.

Movement and a sense of self

As children learn to independently control different parts of their bodies, they are developing their awareness of their own bodies, learning that they are separate from other people, and expressing power. Independent movement—being able to pick up an object, walking, throwing a ball through a hoop—and the accompanying sense of freedom such movement brings, is a major milestone in a child's development in terms of how they feel about themselves. Children can develop self-confidence through mastering motor skills such as grasping, walking or running; through movement, they can discover that they are capable of learning new skills and gathering new information, which can increase their interest in and curiosity about trying new things, motivating them to master new skills.

When children move and others respond, they are discovering that their actions can have an effect on other people and on the world around them, which in turn supports their own sense of power and efficacy. Child development experts have found that children who are physically active and experience success in movement activities improve their self-esteem and have a more positive view of themselves (Liu, Wu and Ming 2015).

Movement and social-emotional skills

As children gain independence through the development of their physical skills, they come in contact with more people. They can choose to move towards or away from others. Children can learn how to make friends through moving together. Movement increases their ability to play with each other and offers them new ways of being with other people. Moving with other people helps children learn the rules of their social worlds.

Movement and exercise are also key strategies in managing joy and happiness as well as stress, anger, anxiety and depression. Whether it's dancing when sharing feelings of joy or banging on a drum when feeling angry, movement helps children express, vent, communicate, build awareness of and ultimately understand and manage their feelings. Through movement, children both experience a wide variety of feelings and quickly learn that these feelings can and do change, especially through being physically active.

Movement and learning

According to Carl Gabbard and Luis Rodrigues (2007), movement encourages brain development in early childhood. As discussed throughout this book, when children move they come in contact with many different textures, shapes, colors and objects. They are getting needed sensory input through increasing their interactions with people and things that help generate the development of neural connections and networks. In addition, they are learning about cause-and-effect relationships and improving problem-solving skills. And children increase their language skills through movement as they come in contact with new objects and build their vocabularies.

Movement can fuel interest and curiosity in children, which in turn can improve their ability to learn, focus and pay attention. Young children learn better when they are physically involved and when lessons include movement.

Movement and health

Physical activity helps children improve their short- and long-term physical health. As many research studies have shown, children (and adults) who are physically active on a regular basis reduce their risk for many diseases and health issues, including heart disease, obesity and diabetes. Children who regularly move are building strength and flexibility in their muscles and bodies, increasing the oxygen to their muscles and brain, and helping maintain a healthy weight. According to a report from the National Institute of Health's Committee on Physical Activity and Physical Education in the School Environment (Kohl and Cook 2013):

> Physical activity reduces the risk for heart disease, diabetes mellitus, osteoporosis, high blood pressure, obesity, and metabolic syndrome; improves various other aspects of health and fitness, including aerobic capacity, muscle and bone strength, flexibility, insulin sensitivity, and lipid profiles; and reduces stress, anxiety, and depression. (p.97)

Movement and overall growth and development

A moving child is a learning, growing and developing child. A moving child is a happier child. We want to promote healthy developmentally appropriate movement activities on a daily basis for our children in order to help with all areas of development. And as we'll soon discuss, music is all about movement!

Standards for physical activity

The American Academy of Pediatrics "Bright Futures" (Hagan, Shaw and Duncan 2008) initiative provides guidelines for physical activity for young children.

Infants 0–11 months	Daily engagement in physical activities with caregivers. Physical activities that support the use of curiosity to explore and interact with what they encounter. Environments that provide engaging opportunities that stimulate them to move. Movements that are appropriate to developmental level and encourage skill-building.
Toddlers 1–2 years	60 minutes or more of unstructured physical activity daily. 30 minutes of structured physical activity daily. No more than 60 minutes of inactivity at a time.
Children 3–5 years	60 minutes or more of unstructured physical activity daily. 60 minutes of structured physical activity daily. No more than 60 minutes of inactivity at a time. Physical activities that focus on skill-building and physical development.

In addition to these guidelines, the Society of Health and Physical Educators (SHAPE) (National Association for Sport and Physical Education 2009) emphasizes that the environments we provide for physical activity should be safe and should encourage movement in both indoor and outdoor settings.

What you can do to promote physical activity and development

Your role is important! The American Academy of Pediatrics (2003) suggests that you can do a number of things to promote healthy physical activity and development: demonstrate a positive attitude towards physical activity; provide environments that are conducive to age-appropriate physical activity; and limit the use of electronics.

Demonstrate a positive attitude

Parents who show enthusiasm for physical activity and exercise can help their children develop a life-long positive attitude towards movement.

This translates into an increase in motor skills; improved physical, cognitive and social development; and increased physical fitness and health and mental health. The patterns and habits that children develop in their early years can last a lifetime.

Provide environments that promote physical activity

It's up to parents and professionals in charge of caring for and teaching young children to provide environments, opportunities and activities that are safe, engaging and developmentally appropriate for physical activity and motor skill learning. This includes opportunities for movement and exercise both indoors and outdoors. Make room in your house for movement and take your children outside to the playground.

Put limits on electronics

There's no avoiding electronics in this day and age—they are everywhere. Controlling your children's use of tablets, phones, computers and so on is a challenge. But it's important to find a balance between the benefits of technology and the costs. A video on a smartphone can help keep our child engaged while we pay the bills, but that child is losing valuable exercise time. Do your best to limit the amount of screen time, especially for very young children, in order to provide opportunities for them to move—and through moving, to learn, grow and develop in all areas.

Music is movement

Many children (and adults!) find it almost impossible not to move when music is playing. Have you ever watched a toddler listening to upbeat dance music? It's as if the music takes control over their bodies and makes them move. They can't fight the urge to dance! And who doesn't love a good, purely felt "toddler dance"? Their legs are planted wide apart on the ground to ensure stability and their arms are outstretched as they bounce up and down to the beat of the music with sheer joy.

I often have the same problem with music taking over my body. Some music reaches deep inside of me and my foot uncontrollably starts tapping, I bob my torso to the beat, and I am flooded with feelings. It's as if I'm under the control of the music and have to move.

Music is movement. Music and movement are inseparable. When we make music we are moving our bodies; we are "musicking." Music makes movement and learning more fun and effective, especially with young children. Music has the power to reach deep inside each of us and stimulate feelings that motivate us to physical action. You could say that music conveys feelings through sound, which in turn inspires us to feel and act on those feelings through…movement and action.

Music can help us feel more connected to, and inside of, our bodies. Music can help us feel physically connected to each other through singing, dancing and playing instruments together. When we move to music together, a special bond can be created between participants.

When a young child seemingly responds instinctively by moving to music, she is doing it for more than the pure joy it inspires. This is not only "music for the sake of music." Musical movement is an ideal way to help children develop their bodies, brains, minds, relationships and culture.

Music for physical fitness and development

Musical movement is physical exercise and, like all forms of exercise, it can help increase children's physical fitness and the development of their motor skills. Dance is an aerobic activity that can build heart health and stamina. Movement to music can help build the strength, balance and coordination needed to become more independent movers. For example, in a simple song like "Head, Shoulders, Knees and Toes" children are not simply learning body parts. They are moving their hands from the tops of their heads to their shoulders to their knees to their toes, strengthening their torsos and increasing their balance while they also improve their ability to listen and follow directions. The activities we call "fingerplays" support the development of fine motor skills as children learn to independently move different sets of fingers together.

Through musical movement, children can build body awareness as they learn to label and independently move different parts of their bodies in different patterns. The Scottish folk song "Aiken Drum" (Ch. 8) and "If You're Happy and You Know It" (Ch. 3) are both great examples of songs that encourage children to point to and/or learn to move specific parts of their bodies in rhythm as directed at specific times.

Including both structured and unstructured music movement times in every child's daily routine is both fun and good for their developing bodies and physical health. Thirty minutes of dancing to "Five Little Monkeys Jumping on the Bed" (Ch. 5) or "Ring Around the Rosie"

(Ch. 3), or participating in a freeze dance, will increase everyone's heart rate and physical fitness!

Musical movements increase sensory input and exploration

Moving to music offers children many opportunities to engage in rich sensory experiences, feeding important brain development in the early years. Through musical movement, children are increasing what they hear, see and feel. They are increasing the quantity and quality of information their brains are receiving and processing. They are building a library based on the input they receive and the cause-and-effect relationships they observe.

Try giving your child a scarf to hold and wave and call up Mozart's *Symphony 40* on your tablet or phone. Your child will be getting auditory input from the music, tactile input from holding the fabric scarf and feeling his body move through space, and visual input from watching a multi-colored scarf move up, down and round and round. He is watching how his movements relate to the music and making adjustments based on what he sees, feels and hears.

Musical movement is a social-emotional experience

When children move to music together, they are developing their social-emotional skills as well as their imaginations and creative abilities. When children move while engaging in musical activities, they are learning to follow directions and work towards a shared goal. Through musical movement, children can experience the joy of being a part of a group and also enhance their self-confidence as they learn to control their bodies, increase their focus and attention, and manage their feelings.

When children move together with other children, they are experiencing the joy of cooperating and working together as a group. Watching the enthusiasm and sense of accomplishment five-year-olds express when they are learning to dance a reel to "Alabama Gal" is priceless. Dancing in a circle and playing "Looby Loo" (Ch. 5) helps children learn to move different parts of their bodies independently, but it also helps them listen to and follow directions while engaged in a group activity.

Freeze dances (see Chapter 3) and other go/stop musical games are great social movement activities. As described in the "Songs, games and activities" section in Chapter 3, children are directed to "go" and "stop" on command as they learn to follow simple directions together. In between the "go" and "stop," however, they have the freedom to dance and move freely. They learn to listen and to control their bodies at specific moments as directed. They learn to manage and contain the excitement of their feelings in order to follow the simple structure of the game. Many young children love leading go/stop movement games, which gives them a sense of power and control as well as responsibility. And don't underestimate the workout they'll get from a fast-paced freeze dance!

Making music and movement a part of your child's daily routine

There is any number of things you as a parent or caregiver can do to include music in your child's daily physical routine. Planned and unplanned musical moments can help you manage your child's development—and can sometimes defuse a challenging or difficult moment.

Everyday musical moments

Schedule some structured movement music time every day. If your child tends to be full of energy when she first wakes up, for example, schedule 10 to 15 minutes of energizing dance before breakfast (unless you need that first cup of coffee before moving at all). Or if your child tends to lag toward the end of the day, add 10 to 15 minutes before dinner. This is a great way to connect with your child, build skills—and get exercise!

Musical movement is a great tool when you need to refocus a distracted child or help a child express angry, anxious or sad feelings. Use unstructured free-play musical movement during difficult moments to help your child vent and you to manage. Or try some marching music to help manage a transition (see more on transitions in Chapter 7). If getting ready for preschool is challenging, try to find a fun energizing song to get everyone feeling ready to face the day!

Find a movement song to help your children learn specific concepts. Teach them "Five Green and Speckled Frogs" (Ch. 6) before you head off for a visit to a nearby pond, or "Old MacDonald" (Ch. 6) if you plan a visit to a children's zoo or a farm.

Musical movement activities are great to use on playdates to help break the ice and get the children engaging and interacting with each other. And try to choose daycares and preschools that weave age-appropriate physical activities into their daily schedule—ideally, activities that include music!

Before you move

As you include music in your daily routines and in your child's life, make sure to keep in mind some important things—the most important being *safety first*.

Always make sure you are providing a safe, open area in which to move and dance, and, as I've mentioned repeatedly, teach your child about personal space (the need to keep a safe distance, generally an arm's length away from other children as they move or dance). If the dancing gets over-exuberant, remind your child of the importance of controlling his body.

Watch out for mental or physical fatigue, and make sure to provide "sit-down" or water breaks as needed. If a child loses interest or simply tires out, offer an opportunity to rest or move to another activity. Too much of a good thing, as the saying goes, can leave a child uninterested in coming back to a given activity.

While you move

As children are moving to music, help them learn appropriate social-emotional skills: maintaining appropriate personal space, taking turns, and not teasing each other based on how they move. Choose songs and activities that are developmentally appropriate to the individual or age group. Some dance activities may need to be adapted for an individual or age group depending on their abilities. For example, if a child is in a wheelchair, change the words of "Ring Around the Rosie" to say "all clap hands" or "all tap knees" or "arms fall down" instead of "all fall down." And while some pop songs are fun to dance to, be careful to make sure that their themes are appropriate for young children.

Balance letting your child practice what she knows with trying new moves and activities. Alternate helping her learn new things with allowing her to explore on her own. Children like to figure things out independently, but sometimes they need us to help.

Children love repetition of songs they know, but they also like the novelty of new skills and activities to master. You can try adding a twist to an old favorite—for example, as I mentioned in Chapter 3, try changing "If You're Happy and You Know It" to "If You're Angry and You Know It." Ramp up the fun meter by providing a prop such as a scarf, a pompom or even a small parachute to the movement activity. If you're in a group, try to scaffold activities (adapt tasks to each child's age and skill level) so that children at all ages and levels can participate together. For example, if the song calls for jumping, offer the "non-jumpers" the opportunity to do knee bends or to pat their knees.

Anything you do to add musical movement to your daily routine will benefit your child—and, if you dance or move along too, it can't hurt your own physical health!

Putting it all together

When we make music or dance, we are physically moving. We are coordinating the movements of our fingers, hands, legs, torsos and mouths to produce patterns and sequences of sound. We are expressing our thoughts and feelings through movement. Whether we are singing, playing an instrument or dancing, we are engaging our physical bodies. And this kind of physical engagement isn't simply fun, it also supports growth and development in a wide range of areas, including cognition, social-emotional skills, self-regulation, sense of self and, of course, physical wellbeing.

SONGS, GAMES AND ACTIVITIES FOR PHYSICAL FITNESS AND DEVELOPMENT

This section includes specific songs and musical activities that you can use to support your child in developing physical fitness and motor skills. The accompanying music and video files can be downloaded from www.jkp.com/voucher using the code BOOMESE.

A wide variety of songs can be used to encourage movement. We've looked at some of these in previous chapters—"Ring Around the Rosie," "If You're Happy and You Know It," and so on. Here we'll look at five categories of movement songs: more *fingerplay songs* to help build fine motor skills through the use of finger movements; more *play songs* that encourage the development of gross motor skills by including large movements; *songs that use props* like scarves, balls and parachutes that help children build coordination; *foot tambourine songs* that help develop body awareness, balance, stamina and coordination; and *hula hoop songs* that help children build focus and learn to contain their movements.

FINGERPLAYS

Purpose

Fingerplays help children build their fine motor skills as they learn to coordinate the movements of their fingers, hands, arms and legs. Fingerplays also have other benefits (as is true for most of the songs included in this book): They help children develop language skills through pairing small movements with words and actions; and they help increase awareness of letter sounds, vocabulary and familiarity with patterns and rhythm of speech. Fingerplays are fun to do in parallel, since everyone can participate at the same time together.

How to

Sit facing your child. Sing through the song as you demonstrate the finger, hand and arm movements. Go slowly at first, encouraging your child to mirror your singing and movements. As he learns the fingerplay, try leaving off the last word or movement of a line and pausing while he tries to remember what's next. After he masters the song, ask him to sing the song for you.

"Itsy Bitsy Spider"

Traditional

The itsy bitsy spider went up the water spout	[make spider movements with hands—right thumb to left index finger, then left thumb to right index finger, 4x]
Down came the rain and	[sprinkle fingers from overhead down to floor]
washed the spider out	[swipe hands from arms crossed in front of body to outstretched at sides]
Out came the sun	[raise arms in overhead in big open semi-circle shape]
and dried up all the rain and the	[sprinkle fingers from floor up over head]
itsy bitsy spider went up the spout again	[repeat first motion of right thumb to left index finger, then left thumb to right index finger, 4x]

"Here Is a Bunny"

Traditional

Note: This is a chant—there is no melody but try to speak the words with a steady beat.

Here is a bunny	[hold up index and middle fingers of right hand in peace sign symbol]
With ears so funny	[wiggle fingers, bending up and down, bending at 2nd joint of fingers]
And here is his hole in the ground	[make circle by joining thumb and index finger of left hand in "OK" symbol]
At the first sound he hears he wiggles his ears	[wiggle fingers, bending up and down, bending at 2nd joint of fingers]
And hops in his hole in the ground!	[insert bunny ears/index and middle fingers of right hand in hole in the ground/circle made with thumb and index finger of left hand]

"There Was a Little Turtle"

Traditional

Note: This is a chant—there is no melody but try to speak the words with a steady beat.

There was a little turtle	[make fist with left hand and hold in front of body]
Who lived in a box.	[hold right hand over left hand fist]
He swam in the water	[make swimming movement with both arms]
And he climbed on the rocks.	[move fingers of right hand over left hand fist]
He snapped at a mosquito.	[bring thumb and fingers together in a snapping motion: open and close fingers of right hand—thumb into rest of fingers]
He snapped at a flea.	[open and close fingers of right hand—thumb into rest of fingers]
He snapped at a minnow.	[open and close fingers of right hand—thumb into rest of fingers]
And he snapped at me.	[open and close fingers of right hand—thumb into rest of fingers]
He caught the mosquito.	[clap hands together]
He caught the flea.	[clap hands together]
He caught the minnow.	[clap hands together]
But he didn't catch me!	[shake head and wag finger in "no" movement]

👍 Personal reflections

I love the simplicity of fingerplays. The only thing you really need is your fingers, hands, arms and legs. I usually put down my guitar or banjo during these moments and just sing and demonstrate the movements. Children usually watch my hands very closely to figure out what to do.

What are your child's favorite fingerplays?

Notes

PLAY SONGS TO BUILD GROSS MOTOR SKILLS

Purpose

Gross motor play songs involve the large muscles in the arms, legs and torso. Think of these as bigger dances that use the bigger body parts and sometimes the entire body. These songs can provide opportunities for both structured and unstructured movement. Structured gross motor songs have specific patterns of movements which children follow for specific periods of time. Unstructured gross motor songs allow for a more open physical expression in response to the music. Think of ballroom dancing as "structured" and dancing at a Phish concert as "unstructured."

Gross motor songs offer opportunities for building physical fitness and skills as well as developing social-emotional, communication and cognitive skills. Many structured gross motor songs focus on specific movements that help build body awareness, balance, coordination and strength in specific body areas.

Structured dances, such as circle dances, reels and partner dances, offer opportunities for helping children to learn to work together in a coordinated manner. Structured gross motor play songs can help children learn to focus, listen, process directions and move as directed as they build their cognitive skills. Structured gross motor songs sometimes have an "imitation" component where one person leads and the group copies or "echoes" their movement. Unstructured dances also offer opportunities for learning social-emotional skills, such as personal space and self-control, but tend to be less demanding in terms of focus.

Gross motor play songs also offer opportunities, as children are moving their bodies through space, to gather, process and act on all the sensory input from what they see, feel and hear.

How to

Make sure your space is safe for dancing and movement. Remind children about any safety concerns—where they should and shouldn't go, not to run when dancing, to always be in control of their bodies—and about maintaining appropriate personal space. Demonstrate the movements as you describe the instructions for the dance. Start slowly at first and increase in speed as your child masters the song. Watch for cues to slow down or repeat an instruction or a modeled movement. And have them slow down or momentarily freeze if they appear to be getting too rambunctious.

"Head, Shoulders, Knees and Toes"

Traditional

Purpose

Children learn to identify different body parts as they exercise and build up their core muscles. They will learn to follow simple directions while matching the speed of the song.

How to

Encourage your children to touch each body part as it is sung. Start singing the song slowly and demonstrating the movements. As they learn the movements and follow along, try singing faster and faster.

Head, shoulders, knees and toes (knees and toes)
Head, shoulders, knees and toes (knees and toes)
Eyes and ears and
Mouth and nose
Head, shoulders, knees and toes (knees and toes)

Variations

- Try varying the speed you sing to keep them literally "on their toes."

- Use the new lyrics I wrote for this song to help children learn about what to wear in the winter! Have them touch the pretend winter clothing items on their bodies as it is sung about.

Hat, scarf, coat and boots (coat and boots)
Hat, scarf, coat and boots (coat and boots)
Ear muffs and mittens keep me warm when I'm cold
Hat, scarf, coat and boots (coat and boots)

HEAD SHOUL-DERS KNEES AND TOES KNEES AND TOES

HEAD SHOUL-DERS KNEES AND TOES KNEES AND TOES

EYES AND EARS AND MOU-TH A-ND NOSE

HEAD SHOUL-DERS KNEES AND TOES KNEES AND TOES

"Looby Loo"

Traditional

Purpose

Children learn to move body parts independently while building their balance, strength and stamina. They learn to follow directions.

How to

Have children stand in a circle facing inward. For each VERSE, model the movements while encouraging them to follow along. For each CHORUS have everybody sing along and dance in-place. The structure of the song is VERSE, CHORUS, VERSE, CHORUS, etc. until you have completed all the VERSES.

VERSE	
You put your right hand in	[everyone puts right hand in circle]
You put your right hand out	[everyone takes right hand out of circle]

cont.

You give your hand a shake, shake, shake	[everyone shakes right hand]
And turn yourself about	[everyone turns around]
CHORUS	
Here we go looby loo	[everyone claps and sings while turning around in a complete circle]
Here we go looby light	
Here we go looby loo	
All on a Saturday night	
VERSE	
You put your left hand in	[everyone puts left hand in circle]
You put your left hand out	[everyone takes left hand out of circle]
You give your hand a shake, shake, shake	[everyone shakes left hand]
And turn yourself about	[everyone turns around]
CHORUS	
Repeat VERSE section using body parts listed below, with CHORUS in between. Right foot Left foot Bottom Whole body [jump into and out of circle]	
CHORUS	

"Hey, Hey Look at Me"

Traditional

Purpose

Children learn to initiate and copy movements. They increase their body awareness, balance and coordination.

How to

Chant the song one time through while demonstrating a movement—clapping, for example. Sing again and encourage your child to copy your movement while chanting with you. Then have your child chant and make up a movement for you to copy. Follow the above pattern by singing along and copying their movement as they sing through the song a second time. Keep taking turns leading and copying movements until everyone in your group has a chance to lead or until you're ready to move on!

Hey, hey look at me	[Make eye contact with your child(ren)]
I am clapping	[Clap hands]
Can't you see	[Continue to clap]
	[Repeat the verse above, this time encouraging everyone to join in with the clapping]
Hey, hey look at me	[Child makes eye contact with participants]
I am _____ [insert the new move]	[Child does movement that she sings about]
Can't you see	[Child continues movement]
	[Repeat the verse above, this time encouraging everyone to join in with the new move]

Variations

Choose movements that demonstrate specific categories:

- Simple motions, like clapping, stomping, jumping, tapping knees.

- Feelings, like happy, sad, mad, scared.

- Things you do in the summer, like swimming, riding a bicycle, eating ice cream.

- Methods of transportation like train, car, bicycle, skateboard.

- Make up your own categories!

"Hickory Dickory Dock"

Traditional

Purpose

Children develop their balance and coordination as they rock from side to side while pretending they are a clock. They also increase their ability to feel and move with a steady beat.

How to

Have your child stand and face you an arm's length away. Some, especially younger children, benefit from your holding their hands across from you. Model rocking side to side and encourage him to copy your movements while chanting the song. You can try to chant the song at different speeds for fun and to increase balance and coordination. Note that for this version there is no melody—but try to speak the words with a steady beat.

Hickory dickory dock
The mouse ran up the clock
The clock struck one
The mouse ran down
Hickory dickory dock

"Skip to My Lou"

Traditional

Purpose

Children increase their physical fitness and motor skills as they march and skip throughout the song.

How to

For the CHORUS section, encourage children to put their hands face down in front of them—waist high. Ask them to march or skip in place with their knees touching their hands on each step. For the VERSE sections, ask them to follow movement directions provided or make up their own movements based on the lyrics. You can also encourage them to make up their own movements for each VERSE based on the lyrics.

CHORUS	
Skip, skip, skip to my Lou,	*[hold hands out at waist-high height with palms facing down and march or skip so knees hit the palms of your hands]*
Skip, skip, skip to my Lou,	
Skip, skip, skip to my Lou,	
Skip to my Lou, my darlin'	
VERSE	
Little red wagon, paint it blue	*[make painting motion with big up and down strokes]*
Little red wagon, paint it blue	
Little red wagon, paint it blue	
Skip to my Lou, my darlin'	
CHORUS	
VERSE	
I lost my partner, what'll I do?	*[look around the room and make "shrugging" movement with arms and shoulders]*
I lost my partner, what'll I do?	
I lost my partner, what'll I do?	
Skip to my Lou, my darlin'	
CHORUS	
VERSE	
Find another one, as pretty as you	*[march or skip around the room]*
Find another one, as pretty as you	
Find another one, as pretty as you	
Skip to my Lou, my darlin'	
CHORUS	
VERSE	
Fly in the buttermilk, shoo, fly, shoo	*[move one arm from side to side in front of your body]*
Fly in the buttermilk, shoo, fly, shoo	
Fly in the buttermilk, shoo, fly, shoo	
Skip to my Lou, my darlin'	
CHORUS	

Variations

There are many variations of this song; some have children dancing alone, some with partners, and some in a circle. For the early childhood years, I prefer to do this song as a free dance with children dispersed randomly around the room and skipping and marching in place.

"Five Little Monkeys Jumping on the Bed"

Traditional

Purpose

Children will increase their physical fitness and motor skills as they jump throughout this popular chant.

How to

Encourage children to jump and act out the chant as directed below. In the interest of safety, I usually direct children, however, *not* to fall down on the "One fell off and bumped his head" part. I instead ask them to just pretend to bump their heads gently with one hand instead of falling. Safety first!

Five little monkeys jumping on the bed	*[jump up and down on floor]*
One fell off and bumped his head	*[gently tap side of head with one hand]*

Momma called the doctor and the doctor said	[hold hand to side of head in pretend phone call motion]
No more monkeys jumping on the bed!	[wag finger in front of body in "no" motion]
[Repeat above words and motions for: 4, 3, 2 and 1 little monkeys]	

Variations

Children love jumping! But some children either have physical challenges that interfere with their ability to jump or have not yet developed the ability to jump. Encourage these children to bend their knees and bounce, tap their knees with their hands, or simply sing along. I always encourage children to chant the "No more monkeys jumping on the bed!" part with me each time through the song.

"Picking Apples from the Tree"

by Jeffrey Friedberg © 2000

Purpose

"Picking Apples from the Tree" helps children build the skills and stamina of alternating their arms over their heads in an "apple picking" motion.

How to

Sing or play a recording of the song and encourage your children to pretend to pick apples during the VERSE. Encourage them to sing along with the CHORUS. Vary singing the song fast and slowly and ask them to identify and follow along with your speed. Encourage them to echo you in the BRIDGE section.

VERSE:
Picking apples from the tree
Picking apples one, two, three
Picking apples from the tree
Won't you pick some apples with me

CHORUS:
Apples are a fruit that grow on a tree
Red and yellow and green won't you
Pick some apples with me

VERSE:
Picking apples from the tree
Picking apples one, two, three
Picking apples from the tree
Won't you pick some apples with me

BRIDGE:
Apple sauce (Apple sauce)
Apple pie (Apple pie)
Apple juice (Apple juice)
Me oh my! (Me oh my!)
Apple sauce (Apple sauce)
Apple pie (Apple pie)
Apple juice (Apple juice)
Me oh my! (Me oh my!)
Eat some pie! (Eat some pie!)

"The Bossy Frog"

by Jeffrey Friedberg © 1999

Purpose

"The Bossy Frog" song helps children increase their physical fitness, coordination and ability to follow directions. Children will engage in a variety of movements including hopping like frogs, putting arms up and down, and tapping different parts of their bodies.

How to

Sing or play a recording of the song and encourage your children to follow along with the movements as directed. I usually encourage them to hop like frogs during the CHORUS and instrumental sections.

CHORUS	
Way down yonder in the cranberry bog	[encourage children to hop like frogs during this section]
Lived a big ol' cranky bossy frog	
He sat on his lily pad all day long	
Singing his very, very bossy song	
MOVEMENT SECTION #1:	
Arms up	[raise arms over head]
Arms down	[lower arms to sides]
Clap your hands	[clap hands]
Touch the ground	[touch the ground]
[Note: sing this section 2x]	
CHORUS	
MOVEMENT SECTION #2:	
Touch your nose	[touch your nose]
Touch your toes	[touch your toes]
Tap your knees	[tap your knees]
Say please	[say "please"]
[Note: sing this section 2x]	
CHORUS	
MOVEMENT SECTION #3:	
Stretch your arms	[stretch arms]
Give a big yawn	[yawn and raise arms over head]

cont.

Tap your head	[tap head with one arm]
Go to bed	[pretend to sleep]
[Note: sing this section 2x]	
CHORUS	

WAY DOWN YON–DER IN THE CRAN–BER–RY BOG LIVED A BIG OL' CRAN–KY

BOS – SY FROG. HE SAT ON HIS LI – LY PAD ALL DAY LONG

SIN – GING HIS VE – RY VE – RY BOS – SY SONG. ARMS UP

(ARMS UP) ARMS DOWN (ARMS DOWN)

CLAP YOUR HANDS (CLAP YOUR HANDS) TOUCH THE GROUND (TOUCH THE GROUND)

"Walking Down the Street"

by Jeffrey Friedberg © 1999

Purpose

"Walking Down the Street" helps children increase their physical fitness, coordination and ability to follow directions. They will engage in a variety of movements including walking, jumping, dancing and tip toeing. In addition, they will stop, turn around and touch the ground on cue.

How to

Sing or play a recording of the song and encourage them to follow along with the movements as directed.

I'm walking down the street	[walking movement]
with my two feet	
I'm walking, I'm walking	
I'm walking down the street	
with my two feet	
I'm walking, I'm walking	
And then I stop, and turn around	[stop and then turn around 1 time]
Everybody touch the ground	[touch the ground]
★ ★ ★ ★ ★ ★	
I'm jumping down the street	[jumping in place]
[Repeat above verse with "jumping" throughout]	
★ ★ ★ ★ ★ ★	
I'm dancing down the street	[dancing]
[Repeat above verse with "dancing" throughout]	
★ ★ ★ ★ ★ ★	
I'm tip toeing down the street	[tip toeing]
[Repeat above verse with "tip toeing" throughout]	

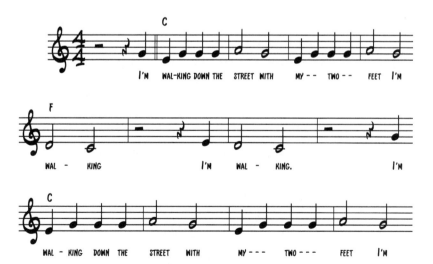

WAL - KING   I'M WAL - KING   AND THEN I

STOP   AND TURN A - ROUND

EV - ERY - BO - DY   TOUCH THE   GROUND.   (I'M)

"A Ram Sam Sam"

Traditional

Purpose

In this Moroccan children's song, children build coordination in their arms. They also learn how to follow directions and learn sequences of movements.

How to

Sing or play a recording of the song and encourage your child to follow your movements. Try singing slowly at first and modeling the movements. I have found most success sitting cross-legged or standing for this song.

A ram sam sam	*[tap right fist on top of left fist 3 times on the word "sam"]*
A ram sam sam	*[tap left fist on top of right fist 3 times on the word "sam"]*
Guli guli guli guli guli	*[put hands together and pretend pull outwards to sides]*
Ram sam sam	*[tap right fist on top of left fist 3 times on the word "sam"]*
★ ★ ★ ★ ★ ★	
A ram sam sam	*[tap right fist on top of left fist 3 times on the word "sam"]*
A ram sam sam	*[tap left fist on top of right fist 3 times on the word "sam"]*
Guli guli guli guli guli	*[put hands together and pretend pull outwards to sides]*
Ram sam sam	*[tap right fist on top of left fist 3 times on the word "sam"]*
A rafiq, a rafiq	*[raise arms up over head and then touch the ground on each "a rafiq"]*
Guli guli guli guli guli	*[put hands together and pretend pull outwards to sides]*

Ram sam sam	[tap right fist on top of left fist 3 times on the word "sam"]
★ ★ ★ ★ ★ ★	
A rafiq, a rafiq	[raise arms up over head and then touch the ground on each "a rafiq"]
Guli guli guli guli guli	[put hands together and pretend pull outwards to sides]
Ram sam sam	[tap right fist on top of left fist 3 times on the word "sam"]

Variations

I also like to teach a variation of this song using rhythm sticks while engaging in the movements. I provide the versions for singing with movements above and for singing with rhythm sticks below.

A ram sam sam	[tap right stick on top of left stick 3 times on the word "sam"]
A ram sam sam	[tap left stick on top of right stick 3 times on the word "sam"]
Guli guli guli guli guli	[put sticks together and pretend pull outwards to sides]
Ram sam sam	[tap right stick on top of left stick 3 times on the word "sam"]
★ ★ ★ ★ ★ ★	
A ram sam sam	[tap right stick on top of left stick 3 times on the word "sam"]
A ram sam sam	[tap left stick on top of right stick 3 times on the word "sam"]
Guli guli guli guli guli	[put sticks together and pretend pull outwards to sides]
Ram sam sam	[tap right stick on top of left stick 3 times on the word "sam"]
A rafiq, a rafiq	[raise sticks up over head and then touch the ground on each "a rafiq"]
Guli guli guli guli guli	[put sticks together and pretend pull outwards to sides]
Ram sam sam	[tap right stick on top of left stick 3 times on the word "sam"]
★ ★ ★ ★ ★ ★	
A rafiq, a rafiq	[raise sticks up over head and then touch the ground on each "a rafiq"]
Guli guli guli guli guli	[put hands together and pretend pull outwards to sides]
Ram sam sam	[tap right stick on top of left stick 3 times on the word "sam"]

👍 Personal reflections

Gross motor play songs are responsible for some of my favorite moments at my concerts when I am performing for children, in my work as a music therapist and when my children were young. I love experiencing the interaction of children increasing their physical fitness and building their physical skills with using their imaginations as they play.

What are your child's favorite gross motor play songs?

Notes

PROP SONGS

Purpose

Props, such as scarves, parachutes and musical instruments, can enhance the movement aspects of a song through giving children something physical to hold and move. Using a prop can help shy children "break the ice" and encourage them to use their bodies more freely during movement activities. Props can also help a highly energized child learn to better manage his feelings, focus his thoughts and control his body through having a physical object on which to focus. Props can help children develop awareness of, focus on and motivate them to move specific parts of their bodies. Many children enjoy manipulating an object in rhythm and the enhanced expression it offers.

How to

Remind children about keeping appropriate personal space when using props. I always instruct children that the props are only for them to hold and not to put in their mouths, on their faces or heads, or touching anyone else's bodies. This will help them keep their bodies safe and the props clean.

Prop songs, especially using a parachute or scarves, are great fun for playdates, parties and in preschool and daycare. (A small, six-foot parachute will require three to six children to hold it in the air.) If you play with a parachute indoors, make sure you have enough room to safely maneuver in a circle. For outdoors, a flat soft surface, such as a grassy area, is optimal. Instruct your children to hold the parachute with their hands and move slowly as directed. Beware of children who love to dive into the middle of the parachute during parachute play. You may want to have children drawn to doing that stand nearer to you so you can remind them of the instructions for your particular activity.

"When the Wind Is Blowing" (scarf song)

by Jeffrey Friedberg © 2010

Purpose

This scarf prop song helps children expand their range of motion and coordination as they move their scarves side to side, up and down and in big circles in the air. It's a great arm workout! It also helps children learn to listen and follow directions from verbal and visual cues.

How to

Start by giving your child a scarf and taking one for yourself. You can use an old bandana, scarf or dish towel, or purchase an inexpensive set of multicolored scarves from a party or school supply store online. Instruct your child to hold the scarf in one corner with one hand. This is a chant without a melody, so I have not provided a song sheet. Simply chant the words with a slow steady beat while demonstrating the movements.

When the wind is blowing I am going	
Side to side	[hold scarf over your head and move side to side]
Side to side	[hold scarf over your head and move side to side]
Side to side	[hold scarf over your head and move side to side]
★ ★ ★ ★ ★ ★	
When the wind is blowing I am going	
Up and down	[move scarf from up over your head to down towards the floor]
Up and down	[move scarf from up over your head to down towards the floor]
Up and down	[move scarf from up over your head to down towards the floor]
★ ★ ★ ★ ★ ★	
When the wind is blowing I am going	
Round and round	[move scarf in big circles in the air in front of your body]
Round and round	[move scarf in big circles in the air in front of your body]
Round and round	[move scarf in big circles in the air in front of your body]

Variations

Encourage your children to make up and demonstrate their own movements for this chant.

"He's Got the Whole World (in His Hands)" (scarf version)

Traditional

Purpose

This variation of the popular American Spiritual uses scarves to demonstrate each object or action in each verse. It helps children develop their coordination to use their hands and arms to manipulate the scarf in a variety of shapes. They will also use their imaginations as they pretend that the scarf is the "world," the "little bitty babies" and the "brothers and the sisters."

How to

Give a scarf to your child and instruct her to copy you as you sing and change shapes with the scarf.

[hold your scarf in front of your body with each hand in a corner so that it drapes down in a square shape]
He's got the whole world
In his hands
He's got the whole wide world
In his hands
He's got the whole world
In his hands
He's got the whole world
In his hands

[scrunch your scarf into a ball with both hands and rock side to side]
He's got the little bitty babies
In his hands
He's got the little bitty babies
In his hands
He's got the little bitty babies
In his hands
He's got the little whole world
In his hands

[hold your scarf with one hand in a corner and wave over your head side to side]
He's got the brothers and the sisters
In his hands
He's got the brothers and the sisters
In his hands
He's got the brothers and the sisters
In his hands
He's got the little whole world
In his hands

He's got the whole wor-ld in his hands. He's got the
whole wor-ld in his hands. He's got the whole wor-ld
in his hands. He's got the whole world in his hands.

"Noble Duke of York" (parachute version)

Traditional

Purpose

"Noble Duke of York" is a great song to use with a parachute, or even a scarf, to help children learn concepts of up, down and halfway up and down, along with developing their marching skills. This song helps them to develop balance, coordination and strength as they practice lifting the parachute up and down and marching while holding it. The song also offers opportunities to learn to listen and follow directions while working as a group.

How to

Have children—at least three, and four or five is better—form a circle. Give them the parachute and have them each hold an edge with two hands. Have them march in a circle, raising and lowering the parachute according to the directions in the song. You can also play this song with children each holding a scarf and doing the movements individually.

Oh, the noble Duke of York	*[everyone holds the parachute around the edge of the circle and marches in a clockwise direction together]*
He had ten thousand men	
He marched them up to the top of the hill	*[instruct everyone to lift the parachute up over their heads]*

And he marched them down again.	[instruct everyone to slowly lower the parachute down towards their knees]
And when you're up, you're up	[instruct everyone to lift the parachute up over their heads]
And when you're down, you're down	[instruct everyone to slowly lower the parachute down towards their knees]
And when you're only halfway up	[instruct everyone to hold the parachute at nose level]
You're neither up nor down.	[raise arms up and then down]

"Marching Round the Levee" (parachute version)

Traditional

Purpose

I have adapted this traditional song for parachute play. Children learn to march while holding onto a parachute. They learn to coordinate the direction and speed of their marching with the song and their peers as they march in a controlled manner in a circle, into the center of the circle, back out to the outside and then change directions.

How to

Have all of the children—at least three, and four or five is better—form a circle. Give them the parachute and have them each hold an edge with one hand. Have them march in a circle, following the directions in the song.

We're marching round the levee	*[everyone holds the parachute around the edge of the circle and marches in a clockwise direction together]*
We're marching round the levee	
We're marching round the levee	
As we have done before	
★ ★ ★ ★ ★	
We're changing our direction	*[everyone changes direction and marches counter-clockwise]*
We're changing our direction	
We're changing our direction	
As we have done before	
★ ★ ★ ★ ★	
We're marching to the middle	*[everyone holds their piece of the parachute up to shoulder height and slowly marches into the middle of the circle]*
We're marching to the middle	
We're marching to the middle	
As we have done before	
★ ★ ★ ★ ★	
We're marching to the outside	*[everyone holds their piece of the parachute up to shoulder height and slowly marches back to the outside of the circle]*
We're marching to the outside	
We're marching to the outside	
As we have done before	

WE'RE MAR – CHING ROUND THE LEV – EE. WE'RE MAR – CHING ROUND THE LEV – EE. WE'RE MAR – CHING ROUND THE LEV – EE LIKE WE HAVE DONE BE – FORE.

FOOT TAMBOURINE SONGS

One of my favorite new prop activities that I just started using in my early childhood music classes and music therapy sessions is "foot tambourine" play. Latin Percussion® makes these wonderful instruments that are small crescent-shaped tambourines with an elastic band that fits over a shoe. Children wear them and then make music with their feet! While these are adult instruments, I have found them to work wonderfully for children aged 3–5 years old.

Purpose
Foot tambourine activities help children develop awareness of their feet, increase motivation to move and build balance, stamina and coordination.

How to
Put a foot tambourine on one or both of a child's feet. Engage in the songs as directed.

- **Freeze dances:** Use foot tambourines for freeze dances to highlight when a child freezes and when they are dancing.

- **Marching, skipping and jumping songs:** Use foot tambourines during marching, skipping and jumping songs to help highlight and focus attention on their movements. See songs above in "Gross Motor Movement" section including "Five Little Monkeys Jumping on the Bed," "Walking Down the Street," "Skip to My Lou," and "Prop Songs," including "Noble Duke of York" and "Marching Round the Levee."

- **Echo games:** Make a short rhythm by stamping your feet and ask your child to echo you. Ask them to make a short rhythm with their feet and copy them.

- **Steady beat feet:** Sing or play a recording of a song and ask your child to "find the beat" of the song with his feet.

HULA HOOP SONGS

Most children five years old and younger don't have the ability to spin a hula hoop around their waist. But that doesn't mean you can't use them musically to increase physical fitness and build motor skills. Hula hoop play needs adult supervision to reinforce the safety of all children and property. I highly recommend not trying hula hoop play on slippery surfaces or with children who are prone to trip over slightly raised objects on the floor.

Purpose

Hula hoops help children focus and contain their movements while also being fun, colorful objects with which to dance.

How to

See below for a variety of fun musical hula hoop activities.

- **Freeze dances:** Spread one hula hoop per person around the room. When the music plays, tell everyone to dance outside the hula hoops. When the music stops, direct them to quickly (but not too quickly) stand inside a hula hoop. You can also try with one hula hoop for every two children. At the end of the song there should be two children inside each hoop. Watch out for some giggling!

- **Lily pads:** Hula hoops help children physically define and learn about personal space. During jumping songs such as "The Bossy Frog Song" or "Five Little Monkeys Jumping on the Bed," ask each dancer to stay in their hoop for the entire song. This is especially helpful to teach about personal space.

- **Hula hoop pass:** Hula hoop pass is recommended for children who are four to five years old and older. The goal is for a group of children to move a hula hoop around a circle—without letting go of each other's hands. Make a circle with four to eight children holding hands. Put your arm through one hula hoop before you hold hands with your neighbor. Put on some fun dance music and try to move the hoop over the person next to you without letting go of your hands. Encourage each child to try to move the hoop over themselves and to their neighbor without letting go of each other's hands. The game can end when the hoop makes its way around the circle—or when the music stops.

Personal reflections

Props are fun and don't have to be expensive. And you can reuse them over and over again—they don't need to have their operating systems upgraded and don't often become obsolete!

I have also found that most children love turning an object into something else. Turning a scarf into the world, a baby or a leaf blowing in the wind opens up an infinite universe of possibilities for a child. It's both a wonderful opportunity to move as well as a creativity-expanding lesson. And in terms of behavior management, I usually keep a couple of "prop" songs in my "back pocket" for moments when my students need a refocusing or regulating moment.

What are your child's favorite prop songs?

What creative ways did your child find to use the props?

Notes

6

LEARNING, LANGUAGE, LITERACY, MATH SKILLS AND SCHOOL READINESS THROUGH MUSIC

Helping Our Children to Be Eager Thinkers, Learners and Problem Solvers

That's a pretty long chapter title—but it's true: music can help young children build a foundation for learning in general; for learning language, literacy and math skills specifically; and for helping children prepare for and manage the transition to elementary school. Music can provide children with meaningful, relevant and developmentally appropriate contact and interaction with sounds, letters, words, numbers and number relationships, patterns, sequences, shapes and colors. Music is filled with math; it is basically subdividing time into smaller units and reassembling them into rhythms. Songs can help children develop their interest in learning as well as learning specific information and concepts.

When children learn through singing and movement, they can increase how well information, skills and concepts are stored, or encoded, as well as recalled. And, equally important, musical experiences can help build their curiosity and confidence in their abilities as well. Basically, learning through music in the early years matters.

I am not a speech pathologist nor a math or reading specialist. I don't pretend to have all the answers for helping with speech and language or learning issues. What I hope to offer here is a way to start developing your understanding of how music can help your children build their learning, language, literacy and math skills through music, and to help you apply strategies that have worked for me in the past.

Each of the topics covered in this chapter could easily have a chapter of its own—but that would have made a much-too-long book! I've clustered them together because each of them represents a part of cognitive development, and for each, how we interact with our children in their infancy and in the ramp-up to preschool and elementary school is critical to that development.

The early years are learning years

The foundation for learning starts young. As with all areas of development discussed so far in this book, experiences matter. From birth—and even before—children are busy gathering information with their senses and bodies. As their brains are actively building neural connections and networks, their minds are building internal libraries of information and concepts. These are important times.

As mentioned throughout this book, in order to learn and grow to the best of their abilities, young children need meaningful sensory and movement opportunities (Libertus and Hauf 2017; Markham and Greenough 2004). They learn from taking in information, processing it, and then acting on it with their bodies. Young brains are busy forming connections based on what they see, hear, smell, taste and touch. They act in response to this sensory input, which generates more sensory feedback. This loop between sensory input and action is continuous.

During the toddler and preschool years, children develop new ways of communicating, thinking and acting on their worlds. They increase their ability to physically grasp and manipulate objects and figure out how they work. They develop the ability to conceive of things not in front of them at the moment, to understand past, present and future and to think of things as part of categories and not just as single objects. They increase their ability to use imaginary play to explore how things and people work and to develop their thinking, reasoning and problem-solving skills.

Children seek to master skills that help them move towards greater independence. My favorite phrase from my youngest daughter, when she was three years old, was "I can do it myself!" When I tried to show her how to do things, she would push me away. She vehemently wanted to figure things out and do them for herself.

Optimal learning experiences during the early years balance our showing and teaching children with letting them learn and explore on their own. We can best help our children learn through setting up age-appropriate and individually appropriate learning experiences that encourage them to explore, analyze and problem-solve with their senses and bodies; we offer the familiar home base for them to return to after exploring, we set limits and boundaries for safety, and we meet their needs responsively.

Curiosity, confidence and creativity are driving forces in how well and much they learn. Nourishing their budding imaginations can help them develop their problem-solving skills and figure out how things work. We want them to feel both secure that their needs will be met and confident in their own abilities to think, learn and do.

Building language, literacy and math skills

The ability to communicate precedes language development. Children's very first way of communicating—crying—is their first way of expressing their needs. Very soon they find other ways to let us know what they want—through eye contact, smiling, frowning, laughing, turning a head away from or towards something, pointing, and so on. While initially reflexive, these are all ways that young children use to communicate, and through which they begin to learn that they can interact with the people in their environment. These ways of communicating are the precursors of language.

Developing language skills

According to the Linguistic Society of America (2012), for children to develop language optimally as they grow, they need to hear meaningful language. Their ability to *understand* speech, or receptive language, precedes their ability to *create* speech, or expressive language. They need to hear us talk and sing to them about what they are seeing and doing and about things that are relevant and interesting to them. This helps them learn, store and make the sounds of their native language. Remember "Meaningful musical moments" from the end of Chapter 2? In addition to helping us bond with our child, we are helping to build a foundation for learning. They are building their vocabulary of words, as well as learning the rhythms and melodies of their language, or prosody.

Whether spoken, signed or expressed otherwise, language is an important part of a child's development.

- Language increases a child's ability to gather and store information and build new skills.

- Language helps children develop new ways to get their needs met.

- Language allows children to express what they are thinking and how they feel.

- Language changes the way children play, increasing the potential for interaction and cooperation.

Developing literacy and math skills

Meaningful, relevant and developmentally appropriate interaction with letters, words, books, shapes and numbers not only builds language skills, it also helps young children build reading, writing and math skills. When learning is relevant to a child, she is more likely to learn skills and concepts which she may then transfer to new situations and environments. When learning is meaningful, children are more likely to develop a positive attitude towards learning in general and towards words, books, reading, numbers and math specifically. We want to foster their curiosity and confidence in their capability to learn.

It is important to talk, read and sing to our children to help them increase their vocabulary and love of words. We want to help them make connections between what they see on the page of a book and their environment.

We want to help them see number relationships, shapes, patterns and sequences in their everyday environment. We want to help them differentiate shapes and learn the directions (up and down, left and right, over and under) so they can eventually understand and differentiate the shapes and lines on a page that make up letters, words, sentences and paragraphs. We want to help them learn that stories have sequences and beginnings, middles and ends.

As mentioned in Chapter 1, auditory processing skills have also been shown to be related to developing early literacy skills (Woodruff Carr *et al.* 2014). Children who were able to hear and match a steady beat at three years old showed improved literacy skills in elementary school. We want to help them build their listening skills as well as their ability to make sense of what they are hearing in order to learn language and to be able to hear language in their heads. When we help our children learn to listen and match simple beats, we are helping them develop their auditory processing and therefore literacy skills.

School readiness

As children prepare to enter the more structured environment of elementary school, helping them be "ready for school" and able to learn to the best of their abilities is not only about what they know and can do; it is also about our creating environments that foster learning that is adapted to their individual needs, skills, interests and abilities (NAEYC 1995). We want to provide meaningful, creative, multi-sensory and action-oriented learning opportunities. We want to adapt learning experiences to meet individual as well as group needs. And we want to do all this while making sure that they have ample opportunity to explore and learn on their own. It's not so simple—this parenting thing!

"School readiness" is also about children's social-emotional competence, their attitude towards learning, and their ability to use and manage their physical selves. We want our children to be able to interact successfully with teachers and other students. We want them to be able to focus and attend. We want them to feel comfortable in, and be able to control, their bodies and manipulate objects. We want them to have a positive attitude towards learning. We want them to be curious about their environments. We want them to be ready, willing and able to be successful, to the best of their abilities, when entering elementary school at the end of the preschool years.

Children love to learn, and it is up to us to help foster this wonderful quality. Music can help.

Music for learning, language, literacy and math

Music is made for learning and for learning how to learn. During the early years, music is quite effective specifically in helping children build their language, literacy and math skills. The many aspects of music discussed throughout this book—rhythm and melody; the use of repetition, patterns and sequences; songs that teach specific skills and concepts; the relationships formed through music; music as a multi-sensory experience; the ability of music to teach across multiple domains simultaneously—all contribute to helping young children learn and learn to love learning.

We've said this before and we'll say it again: When intentionally, constructively and purposefully provided, music offers benefits across the board—quality sensory input for hearing, sight and touch; opportunities to learn cause-and-effect relationships; opportunities to analyze and solve problems in a child's environment; opportunities to use one's imagination and think creatively; and opportunities for building a healthy sense of self, emotional connectedness and the ability to work cooperatively with others. When we help children access their "musical brains," we are helping them learn to the best of their abilities. And when we scaffold musical activities to meet and balance the many different learning needs and experiences of individuals and groups, we are helping all learners to have successful learning experiences at the same time.

Language and music

Music offers children opportunities to meaningfully connect and interact with language in developmentally appropriate ways that are relevant to their lives. Musical conversations, in addition to helping us bond with our children (see Chapter 2), encourage children in their efforts to build a library of sounds and words, as well as develop an understanding of the melody, rhythms and patterns of speech, and rules of their native language. We can playfully vocalize sounds back and forth in a musical manner with infants or engage in silly spontaneous singing of words with our toddlers and preschoolers. Through the singing back and forth, we are helping them learn the sounds and process of using language and having conversations.

A toddler can build his vocabulary as well as his fluency and recall of language by proudly finishing the line of a song that we start singing by adding the last word on his own. When a preschooler sings the same song over and over and over again, she is practicing language in a playful manner. Repetition is an important part of the learning process. When children take songs they have mastered and begin to vary the words or themes, they are using their imaginations and developing their creativity. I have endless memories of young clients of mine taking songs that they have learned and playfully changing the words to reflect what they are thinking and feeling. I didn't have to be a genius to figure out what was on my five-year-old client's mind when he sang "Old MacDonald had a train yard"! When children sing for and with each other, they are engaging in meaningful language and communication that will improve both their language and their social skills. This is all-important musical play for learning across multiple developmental domains, including language.

Fill-in songs like "Old MacDonald" (Ch. 6), mentioned above, and "Ain't No Bugs" (Ch. 6) and "Green Berry Tree" (Ch. 7), prompt children to develop their understanding of categories and to build their speech recall and fluency skills. These songs are structured so that the singers have to think of a creature that fits the category of each song (a farm animal for "Old MacDonald" and "Green Berry Tree," a bug for "Ain't No Bugs") and fill it in at the appropriate time during the song. Music is forgiving and flexible, in that songs can be slowed down or sped up to meet an individual child's abilities. But the ultimate goal should be to "fill in" the words while singing at a steady speed to demonstrate true learning of information and skills through fluency of expression and ease of recall.

Echo songs, such as "No More Pie" (Ch. 3) and "Down by the Bay" (Ch. 6), are great language-building activities. When presented at an individual and developmentally appropriate level, most children love to listen, remember and repeat short phrases sung to them as they build their language and memory skills. Such songs provide a fun social musical experience that offers immediate success, since children have to sing back words and match rhythms and melodies that have literally just been sung to them.

Call-and-response songs are similar but a little more complicated, in that children learn to sing a repeated specific word or phrase in response to a changing word or phrase sung by someone else (a "call"). "John the Rabbit" (Ch. 7) is a fun call-and-response song. Call-and-response songs help children learn to focus on and sing their own unique part, despite hearing a different part immediately before their turn to sing. This is a little more linguistically and cognitively challenging than echo songs.

From simple nursery rhymes to fill-in songs to echo songs to call-and-response songs to silly songs to tongue twisters to story songs, music is a language workshop.

Literacy and music

From focusing on and picking out specific instrument sounds when listening to music to matching a beat when playing together to echoing songs sung to them, children are developing their auditory discrimination and processing skills. As mentioned earlier, research by Woodruff Carr *et al.* (2014) has demonstrated that children who have better auditory processing skills, as demonstrated by being able to hear and play a steady beat at age three, have better literacy skills when they get to elementary school. When we read and think, we are hearing the sounds in our heads. As children learn to discriminate among different sounds, focus their hearing and differentiate auditory noise from relevant sounds, they are also building their auditory processing and literacy skills.

Songs can also help children develop an appreciation for words, both spoken and written. There are many song structures that provide playful ways to interact with and make meaningful contact with words. And songs that help children use all of their senses and their bodies to learn about directions, shapes and patterns and sequences of sounds help prepare them to learn how to decipher written letters, words and patterns and sequences of words. For example, "Noble Duke of York" (Ch. 5) helps them learn about up, down and halfway up and down. As they learn to read, children will need knowledge of these concepts of direction to decode specific words and what they see on the page. Young children can build a foundation for future literacy skills from these experiences.

There are, of course, specific songs that help develop letter and word skills. "The ABC Song" (Ch. 6)is probably the most popular alphabet learning song in the USA. Children proudly learn their letters through singing this song over and over and over again!

Fingerplays, in addition to helping develop fine motor skills, are great for helping children learn the sequence of beginnings, middles and ends of stories. As mentioned previously, fingerplays are basically short simple stories that are accompanied by finger, hand, arm and leg movements. For example, in "Itsy Bitsy Spider"(Ch. 5), through pretending their hands are spiders, the rain, and the sun, children learn a story sequence: a spider climbs; it rains; the spider gets washed out; the sun dries the rain; and the spider climbs up the spout again. (I also think that the "Itsy Bitsy Spider" song helps children learn the value of perseverance, as the spider climbs up the spout triumphantly after having been initially "washed out." It's really a song about resilience in the face of repeated challenges, right?)

Story songs, which offer children many opportunities to develop an appreciation of words and reading, are basically stories set to music. They differ, however, from pure stories in that the musical elements in the telling of the story, such as rhythm, melody and repetition, are integral to the song and help imbue it with meaning in a different way than a story on its own. This isn't meant to devalue stories but rather to share how story songs are different due to the integration of music.

For example, the story song "The Fox" is a song about a fox family and a farmer and their perennial conflict over resources (the fox needs to feed his family and the farmer needs to protect his animals so he can also feed his family). Each verse repeats the same melody, which serves as a familiar container for the story as it progresses. The rousing melody propels us forward and provides energy to the song. The repetition of words in the fourth and sixth lines invites the listener to sing along, even if they don't know the rest of the song. It also reinforces those words as important to the story.

Here is the first verse of the song:

The fox went out on a chilly night,
he prayed to the Moon to give him light,
for he'd many a mile to go that night
before he reached the town-o, town-o, town-o,
he had many a mile to go that night
before he reached the town-o.

Math and music

Music is math. As mentioned in the beginning of this chapter, on a basic level music is essentially subdividing sound and time into shorter and longer units, adding and subtracting these units, and making patterns and sequences that communicate feelings and ideas. When children learn music, they are intuitively learning mathematical relationships and concepts—they are learning to count, to add and subtract, to divide, and to recognize, memorize and create patterns and sequences.

There are also many children's songs that specifically help children learn about and develop an appreciation for numbers and develop counting skills. "Five Green and Speckled Frogs" (Ch. 6) and "Five Little Monkeys on the Bed" (Ch. 5) help children learn to count down from five to zero. "1, 2, Buckle My Shoe" (Ch. 6) helps children learn to count up to ten.

According to Geist (2018), foundational math concepts, including one-to-one correspondence, counting and discriminating more and less, can be learned through music. Learning to keep an even steady beat helps children learn that one sound equals one beat. They can learn to tap one beat on a tambourine for one beat in a song. When children learn to copy rhythmic patterns, they are learning to count and repeat short numbers of sounds. They can also learn about the concept of more and less through analyzing whether sounds have more or less volume, beats or speed.

Music and school readiness

Music helps all children—children who are different types of learners, children who have unique abilities and interests—develop the skills they need as they prepare to enter elementary school. Below are several important ways that music can help prepare children for entering elementary school. And a reminder that school readiness, as mentioned earlier, is also about what parents, teachers and communities do to help all learners engage at their level of skill, ability and interest. It is up to us to provide learning opportunities that meet the needs of all children.

Developing a positive attitude toward learning

Music can help children develop one of the most valuable attributes of all, a positive attitude toward learning. Singing can help develop an interest in and curiosity about words and numbers, as well as many other concepts in the world. Children who learn to count down from five when singing "Five Little Ducks" are more likely to react with excitement when they find they are able to generalize this information to other situations, such as when they hear a countdown for a rocket launch. They are more likely to look for and explore their worlds for these relationships such as seeing numbers on adjoining houses go up by twos. And a child learning to recognize colors through dancing with scarves to "Jenny Jenkins" (Ch. 6) is learning, as children love to learn, through using their senses, movement and play.

Learning cause and effect

Music offers a multitude of opportunities to explore cause-and-effect relationships and solve problems, two critical skills for school readiness. I love watching children explore how to make sounds with the triangle musical instrument. They often start by holding the metal triangle in their hands, tapping it with the striker and making a dull thud sound. Next they often try holding the string and striking it again, producing a sustained ringing tone. If left to their own devices, they usually go back and forth several times, comparing the different sounds and deciding which they like best at that particular musical moment. As much as I am driven to jump in and show them how they are "supposed" to play it, I try to back off and let them explore and figure it out for themselves. They are developing their ability to analyze and make judgments based on their experiences. They are also developing their ability to use their creativity in the service of problem solving and often come up with novel out-of-the-box solutions.

Using imagination and creativity

Music helps children engage their imaginations and use dramatic play in the service of learning. During movement songs, as they hop like frogs, jump like monkeys, fly like birds and swim like fish, they are getting into a role and inhabiting the animal; they are exploring how it might move and feel. When they use instruments to mimic the sounds of the rain and wind, they are learning about and exploring, through play and movement, different aspects of weather.

Developing social skills

Music can help children develop the social skills they need to successfully interact with teachers and students. Children can learn to take turns and work cooperatively through passing games and circle dances. They can learn to both listen and lead through echo songs. They can learn to wait their turn through gross motor musical games. These foundational skills will help them as they enter school and have to work more cooperatively.

Developing physical skills

Music can help children develop physical skills that can help them be more successful in school. As they learn to engage in fingerplays and manipulate musical instruments, they are building fine motor skills, which are increasingly important as children have to learn how to use computers and other small devices. Musical activities including dance, marching songs and playing instruments offer opportunities for important daily exercise. Getting enough exercise improves oxygen intake and physical fitness, which can in turn contribute to focus, self-esteem and managing difficult feelings.

Developing memory and concept awareness

Songs and musical activities can help children learn and remember information and concepts. Pairing information—lyrics—with music reinforces the information and concepts in the song. The combination of melody, rhythm, harmony, timbre, articulation, dynamics, tempo, rhyming, repetition, social connectedness, emotional expression and movement all facilitate the encoding of memories, learning information and building knowledge of concepts. Keeping a steady beat while singing can help increase fluency and recall of information and demonstrate true learning. Who remembers learning the song "The Fifty Nifty" in second grade? This song has been used in elementary schools throughout the USA for years to help children learn the names of all the states in alphabetical order.

Putting it all together

Music is made for learning how to learn, generally, and helping children develop language, literacy and math skills, specifically. Music offers opportunities for meaningful and relevant exposure to letters, words and numbers. Music engages senses, bodies and minds in the service of learning as well as in storing and transferring information and skills. Music is a fun, creative and playful way to learn that also builds confidence and curiosity in learning.

To help our children get ready for the transition to school, we can encourage them to use music to develop the skills, abilities and attitudes they need, but we can also create home learning environments that meet their individual needs, abilities and interests. We can use music to help prepare our children socially, emotionally, physically and cognitively for school. And musical activities can be easily adapted and scaffolded to engage both our individual child and groups of children at a variety of levels of knowledge, skill and ability at the same time once they enter school.

SONGS, GAMES AND ACTIVITIES FOR THINKING, LEARNING, LITERACY, MATH AND LANGUAGE DEVELOPMENT

This section includes specific songs and musical activities that you can use to support your child's thinking, learning, literacy, math and language development. As with all music, these songs also help children learn across all areas of development. Try singing them for and with your children as well as asking them to sing them for you. The accompanying music and video files can be downloaded from www.jkp.com/voucher using the code BOOMESE.

COUNTING SONGS

"1, 2, Buckle My Shoe"

Traditional

Purpose

In this fun counting song, your child learns to count up by two numbers at a time to 10. He can also learn a rhyme for each even number.

How to

You can teach the song by singing it slowly in its entirety or in echo. To teach in echo, sing each line (or half of each line if he is having difficulty remembering and repeating the entire line) and ask your child to echo you.

Note: This is a chant—there is no melody but try to speak the words with a steady beat. Some people sing "big fat hen" instead of "once again" for the last line.

> *1, 2, buckle my shoe*
> *3, 4, shut the door*
> *5, 6, pick up sticks*
> *7, 8, lay them straight*
> *9, 10, once again*

Variations

After your child has learned the song, try singing each line and leaving off the rhyme word at the end and encouraging your child to fill in the rhyme. For example, you sing "1, 2, buckle my..." and encourage your child to find a rhyme for the number 2. Your child may come up with his own creative last words for each line if he doesn't remember the word of the song—or if he's feeling particularly silly that day!

Personal reflections

I like to help children learn this song while they are marching to a steady beat. I find this helps them with their fluency and word recall...and it's fun!

What are your children's or students' favorite counting songs?

Notes

"Five Green and Speckled Frogs"

Traditional

Purpose

This song is a fun way to help your child learn to count down from five. In addition, she can jump like a frog while singing, making it also a gross motor play song.

How to

Instruct your child to jump throughout the song while singing or you encourage them to act out the actions and only jump on the word "jump." Below I will give movements to act out the song. Pause after each verse and ask her to try to figure out how many frogs are left on the log since one just jumped into the pool.

Five green and speckled frogs	
Sitting on a speckled log	*[children sitting in chairs or on floor on pretend log]*
Eating some most delicious bugs, yum yum!	*[children pretend to eat bugs and then shout "yum yum" at end of line]*
One jumped into the pool	*[you can assign one child to jump or have everyone jump once]*
Where it was nice and cool	
Then there were only four green and speckled frogs, glub glub!	*[children shout "glub glub." Then ask children how many frogs are left as one just jumped into the pool]*

cont.

[Repeat with four frogs]	
[Repeat with three frogs]	
[Repeat with two frogs]	
[Repeat with one frog, finishing "Then there were no more green and speckled frogs"]	

FIVE GREEN AND SPECKLED FROGS SIT-TING ON A SPECKLED LOG. EA-TING SOME MOST DE-LI-CIOUS

BUGS (YUM, YUM). ONE JUMPED IN-TO THE POOL WHERE IT WAS NICE AND COOL.

NOW THERE ARE FOUR GREEN AND SPEC-KLED FROGS (GLUB, GLUB).

👍 Personal reflections

If you're looking for a particularly funky version of this song, Adam Falcon sings it on my album "15 Songs Every Kid Should Know (and Will LOVE!)."

How did "Five Green and Speckled Frogs" go?

How did "Five Green and Speckled Frogs" go?

Notes

"Over in the Meadow"

Traditional

Purpose

This fun story song helps children learn to count up to five while building their vocabulary of animals along with building rhyming skills and a love for language play.

How to

Sing the song for your child to familiarize them with the story, structure and rhymes. Each time through, pause at the number of animals part and ask your child what number is next. You can also remind them of how many animals were in the previous verse. Next time you sing it, leave off the last word of each line and ask your child to try to remember the word or to find another rhyming word that fits.

I have adapted the song with my own lyrics. You can use these or find the more traditional lyrics online.

> *Over in the meadow by the pond in the sun*
> *Lived an old mother frog and her little froggie, one;*
> *"Hop!" said the mother. "I hop," said the one,*
> *So she hopped and was happy by the pond in the sun.*
>
> *Over in the meadow in the sky so blue,*
> *Flew an old mother eagle and her little eaglets, two;*
> *"Fly" said the mother. "We fly," said the two,*
> *So they flew and were happy in the sky so blue.*
>
> *Over in the meadow on a leaf on a tree,*
> *Crawled an old mother beetle and her little beetles, three;*
> *"Crawl!" said the mother. "We crawl," said the three,*
> *So they crawled and were happy on a leaf on a tree.*
>
> *Over in the meadow on the banks of the shore,*
> *Lived an old mother crab and her little crabbies, four;*
> *"Snap!" said the mother. "We snap," said the four,*
> *So they snapped and were happy on the banks of the shore.*
>
> *Over in the meadow in a big bee-hive,*
> *Lived an old mother bee and her little bees, five;*
> *"Buzz!" said the mother. "We buzz," said the five,*
> *So they buzzed and were happy in their big bee-hive.*

Note: Most versions go up to 10 or 12 creatures. Feel free to make up your own additional verses or use the traditional ones available online.

👍 Personal reflections

Story songs are great for teaching concepts but they are also great for car trips and bedtimes. They help children focus and regulate their minds and bodies.

What fun new verses did you and your child come up with?

Notes

ALPHABET AND SPELLING SONGS

"The ABC Song"

Traditional

Purpose

Children learn to sing the letters of the alphabet as well as a song that they can share socially with most young children.

How to

Most children love singing "The ABC Song" and actually seem to absorb it rather than having to actively learn it. Sing it slowly together. Then try to sing it but leave off a letter or a couple of letters and let your child fill in the blanks, i.e. "A, B, C, _, E, F, _." After trying this several times, ask your child to try and sing it for you.

(to the tune of "Twinkle, Twinkle, Little Star")

A, B, C, D
E, F, G
H, I, J, K
L, M, N, O, P
Q, R, S
T, U, V
W, X, Y and Z
Now I know my ABCs
Next time won't you sing with me

👍 Personal reflections

A little children's music trivia—"The ABC Song" also shares the same melody with "Baa, Baa, Black Sheep" and "Twinkle, Twinkle Little Star."

Describe your "ABC Song" experiences.

Notes

"H-E-L-L-O"

by Jeffrey Friedberg © 2008

Purpose

"H-E-L-L-O" helps children learn to spell the word "hello" along with learning the social-emotional skill of "greetings" and helping with managing transitions.

How to

I have found the best way to teach this song is to sing it slowly and encourage each child to shout "hello" in echo at the appropriate time. Try singing it consistently in the morning or when your child returns from preschool or a playdate.

> *Put your hand in the air and*
> *wave it up there*
> *Everybody shout hello (hello!)*
> *Put your hand in the air and*
> *wave it up there*
> *Everybody shout hello (hello!)*
> *H - E - L - L - O*
> *Is the way to spell hello*
> *H - E - L - L - O*
> *Everybody shout hello (hello!)*
> *Put your hand in the air and*
> *wave it up there*
> *Everybody shout hello (hello!)*

👍 Personal reflections

While I don't believe in pushing children too early to learn how to spell, read and write, I do think songs like this help them develop an awareness and appreciation of letters as the building blocks of words.

What are your favorite hello songs to use with your children?

How has using a hello song helped your child manage transitions and learn greetings?

Notes

CATEGORY AND FILL-IN SONGS

"Ain't No Bugs"

Traditional

Purpose
This fill-in song is a great way for children to learn about the category of "bugs" while developing an appreciation for words and language. They will build their rhyming skills and their vocabulary while having fun singing a silly song.

How to
Sing the first verse as written. On each subsequent verse, ask them to fill in a name of a bug instead of singing the word "bug" and a rhyme for their "bug." For example:

[First time]
There ain't no bugs on me
There ain't no bugs on me
There may be bugs on some of you mugs
But there ain't no bugs on me

There ain't no [ask child to fill in name of bug]…on me
There ain't no [same bug as above]…on me
There may be [same bug as above] [rhyme about what bug is doing]
But there ain't no bugs on me

[Examples]
There ain't no bees on me
There ain't no bees on me
There may be bees eating some cheese
But there ain't no bees on me

There ain't no flies on me
There ain't no flies on me
There may be flies eating apple pies
But there ain't no flies on me

Each subsequent time through the song, encourage them to choose a bug and then find a rhyme for the bug they chose. You can give them choices of bugs and rhymes if they are having difficulty coming up with one on their own. You can also help them start their rhymes and let them finish with a fun rhyming word. Repeat several times with different bug names. I like to end by singing the first verse again.

👍 Personal reflections

This is a great song to relieve boredom on long car trips or while having to wait for something. It not only teaches rhyming skills and bug names but helps build an appreciation and love for words and language.

What are some bugs and rhymes you and your children came up with?

Notes

"Old MacDonald"

Traditional

Purpose

This favorite fill-in song is a fun way for children to learn about the category of "farm animals," increase recall of words that fit that category, and increase fluency by singing sounds of animals in tempo with the song while developing an appreciation for words and language.

How to

Sing the song and pause on the "and on his farm he had a _____" part and wait for your child to fill in the name of a farm animal. Encourage them to fill in the sound of the animal on the "with a ___ ___ here and a ___ ___ there" part. Some children may need help understanding and knowing which animals fit the category of farm animal. You can help them learn through providing some choices, i.e. "cow or sheep," for them to choose from.

Old MacDonald had a farm	
E-I-E-I-O	
And on his farm he had a _____	*[ask child to fill in name of farm animal]*
E-I-E-I-O	
With a ___ ___ here and a ___ ___ there	*[ask child to make sound of chosen farm animal]*
Here a ___ there a ___	
Everywhere a ___ ___.	
	Note: Repeat above lyrics and ask your child(ren) to fill in with other farm animals and the sounds they make.
[Last time through end with:]	
Old MacDonald had a farm	
E-I-E-I-O	

Variations

You can sing this song with categories other than "farm" animals, e.g. "Old MacDonald had a City," and ask the children to fill in things that are found in a city that make sounds, such as a bus or subway train.

Personal reflections

This is one of the most popular children's songs I have encountered. Children appear to love scanning the files in their brains to come up with animal names and sounds. I try to never underestimate the pride and confidence that children can feel when they come up with an animal and accompanying sound that fits.

What are some animals you and your children came up with?

Notes

"I Am a Leaf"

by Jeffrey Friedberg © 2018

Purpose

Children learn about how leaves on certain deciduous trees change color and fall down in the Fall. As they wait for the word "down," they are building their listening skills and ability to follow directions. They also learn about the directions of up and down.

How to

Discuss with your child about how leaves on deciduous trees change colors in the Fall and fall down. Ask them what colors the leaves change from and to. Show them the colors of green, yellow, red, orange and brown. Explain how leaves start as green but change colors on many trees in the Fall.

Show them photographs or actual leaves that are green and others that have changed color.

Remind them how to safely use a scarf, i.e. practice good personal space by keeping their scarves an arm's length away from each other, do not touch anyone else with their scarf and do not put it on their face or head. Encourage them to hold the scarf in their hands and pretend it's a leaf on a tree waving side to side in the breeze. Tell them that when they hear the word "down" they should throw their leaf up in the air and watch it fall to the ground. Repeat the song several times.

Note: This is a chant—with no melody. Speak the words with a steady rhythmic beat.

> *I am a leaf*
> *holding on to my tree*
> *Spring and summer*
> *waving so free,*
>
> *In Fall I turn red, yellow,*
> *orange or brown*
> *Then it's time for*
> *me to fall "DOWN!"*

COLOR SONGS

"Jenny Jenkins"

Traditional

Purpose
I adapted this traditional folk song to help children learn their colors while singing and dancing. They also develop the ability to listen, follow directions and make up a silly dance.

How to
This song is fun to sing on a playdate or in a preschool with a group of children. I preface the song by telling them that this is a "silly dance contest" and that I want to see which color is the silliest. Note that here are no actual "winners" in this contest. Everybody wins just by participating.

Ask all the children to sit on the floor. Instruct them that when they hear you sing a color that they are wearing then they should stand up and do a silly dance. Ask them to sit down before the next verse. You can also give out different-colored scarves and ask them to stand up and dance when they hear you sing the color of the scarf they are holding. For the last verse of the song, ask everyone to stand up and dance.

Note: Feel free to mix up the order of color verses and to make up your own rhymes for the colors.

> *Will you wear red oh my dear oh my dear*
> *Will you wear red Jenny Jenkins*
> *Oh I won't wear red 'cause I'll never go to bed*
> *I'll buy me a foldy-roldy, tildy-toldy*
> *Seek-a-double, use-a-cozza roll to find me*
> *Roll, Jenny Jenkins, roll*
>
> *Will you wear green oh my dear oh my dear*
> *Will you wear green Jenny Jenkins*
> *Oh I won't wear green everybody will scream*
> *I'll buy me a foldy-roldy, tildy-toldy*
> *Seek-a-double, use-a-cozza roll to find me*
> *Roll, Jenny Jenkins, roll*
>
> *Will you wear blue oh my dear oh my dear*
> *Will you wear blue Jenny Jenkins*
> *Oh I won't wear blue it's the color of my shoe*
> *I'll buy me a foldy-roldy, tildy-toldy*
> *Seek-a-double, use-a-cozza roll to find me*
> *Roll, Jenny Jenkins, roll*
>
> *Will you wear yellow oh my dear oh my dear*
> *Will you wear yellow Jenny Jenkins*
> *Oh I won't wear yellow it's a little too mellow*
> *I'll buy me a foldy-roldy, tildy-toldy*
> *Seek-a-double, use-a-cozza roll to find me*
> *Roll, Jenny Jenkins, roll*
>
> *[Note: everyone dances for this verse]*
> *Will you wear rainbow oh my dear oh my dear*
> *Will you wear rainbow Jenny Jenkins*
> *Rainbow I won't wear, it's the color of my hair*
> *I'll buy me a foldy-roldy, tildy-toldy*
> *Seek-a-double, use-a-cozza roll to find me*
> *Roll, Jenny Jenkins, roll*

Personal reflections

There are many different versions of this song. In the folk tradition, I am pretty sure I have slightly altered the lyrics, melody and chords to fit with my style of singing and playing. Feel free to make up your own personalized version that works for you and your child!

Also, I love the silliness of this song. Some children love getting up and dancing in a silly manner and others are more reserved. For children who are more shy, I either encourage them to dance from a sitting position or I get up and dance with them. You can also try singing the colors of the more exuberant dancers to "break the ice" and get the silly dance juices flowing.

Have you used "Jenny Jenkins" with your children to teach colors as well as following directions and moving?

Notes

"The Big Ship Sails Through the Alley Alley O" (colored scarf version)

Traditional

Purpose

Here's another folk song that I adapted to use to teach children their colors while pretending they are big ships sailing on the sea. They are also learning a mode of transportation, ships and the name of one of the 12 months, September. You can also use this song as a jumping-off point to help them learn about transportation or the months of the year.

How to

Hand out different-colored scarves to each child seated in a group, or give one child a pile of colored scarves. When you sing about a specific color, have the child with that color (or ask the child with the pile of scarves to pick up that color) stand up and sail around the room and return to you at the end of the verse. You can also create an "alley" for them to sail around and return to you, i.e. two chairs that they have to sail around.

Oh the big ship sails through the Alley Alley O,
the Alley Alley O, Alley Alley O,
Oh the big ship sails through the Alley Alley O,
On the last day of September.

Oh the [choose a color to sing here] ship sails through the Alley Alley O,
the Alley Alley O, Alley Alley O,
Oh the [choose a color to sing here] ship sails through the Alley Alley O,
On the last day of September.

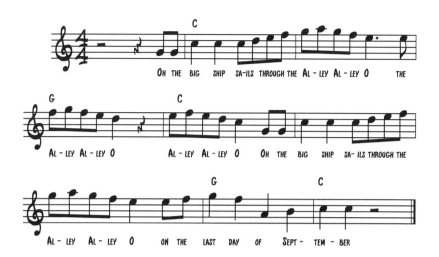

👍 Personal reflections

Many children love pretending that they are cars, trains, airplanes and ships. Through using their imaginations and moving, they are primed to learn many things, including colors, modes of transportation and the months of the year!

How have you adapted this song in your home or classroom?

Notes

ECHO SONGS

"Down by the Bay"

Traditional

Purpose

As mentioned for "No More Pie" (Ch. 3), echo songs help children learn to lead and follow directions. But they also can help increase focus and build memory and language skills. Through listening, remembering and repeating instantly what they just heard, they are able to have successful experiences as they learn and make new sounds, words and rhymes while repeating short phrases that they just heard.

How to

Sing a line of the song and ask your child to echo you immediately using the same words, rhythms and melody. For the second-to-last line ("Did you ever see a _____ _____ a _____?") help your child choose an animal and action that rhyme. For example, "Did you ever see a snake eating a birthday cake?"

Note: The leader sings the part in the left column and the "echoer" imitates with the part in the right column.

Leader: Down by the bay	(Echoer: *Down by the bay*)
Where the watermelons grow	(*Where the watermelons grow*)
Back to my home	(*Back to my home*)
I dare not go	(*I dare not go*)
For if I do	(*For if I do*)
My mother will say	(*My mother will say*)
Did you ever see a _____ _____ a _____?	
Down by the bay!	

Note: Fill in the blanks with an animal and an action—for example:

- duck driving a truck
- mouse living in a house
- cat wearing a hat
- frog dancing on a log.

👍 Personal reflections

If you're feeling adventurous, "Down by the Bay" sounds great accompanied by the ukulele. You'll only need to learn three chords and then you're ready to go! And you can pick up a decent-quality ukulele for $50 which can last a lifetime.

How was your "echo song" experience?

Notes

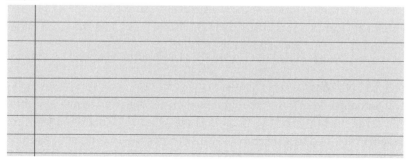

AUDITORY DISCRIMINATION SONGS AND ACTIVITIES

Musical instrument bingo

Auditory discrimination activity

Purpose
Help your children build their auditory discrimination skills through identifying musical instruments by their sounds. This game helps them build their ability to listen, match a sound with an instrument and complete a simple task of putting a chip on a picture of that instrument.

How to
"Musical instrument bingo" games are available for purchase online or you can make your own. If making your own, I recommend making a simple version. First, make a playlist of songs or videos demonstrating different instruments. There are many quality videos of demonstrations of musical instruments available for free on YouTube. Then make a "key" sheet with pictures of the different instruments in your playlist. Then play the songs or videos and point to each corresponding instrument picture on your "key" sheet. Then play each video but let your child hear the audio and not see the video. Ask them to name or point to the picture of the instrument on the key sheet.

If you want to get more sophisticated, you can make up "bingo" cards with different patterns of illustrations of instruments. Each card should have pictures of instruments (in different orders for each card) in three rows of three instruments each. Cut out discs of cardboard, or use other objects to cover each square, and give them out to the children to put on their squares when they hear one of their instruments played. Play a song or video of an instrument but only let them hear the audio (do not show them the video). If they have a picture of the instrument, tell them to cover it up. They "win" if they get a row of three instruments across, down or diagonally. As with any game, song or activity in this book, make sure the small parts are appropriate for your child's age and ability.

👍 Personal reflections
This actual bingo game is recommended for children four to five years old and older. But you can start helping children learn to focus and learn to develop their auditory discrimination skills at a very young age. As they

learn to identify musical instruments by their sounds, try asking them to pick out instruments from songs that come on the radio randomly. My kids used to love doing this.

What instruments can your child identify by sound?

Notes

Name the tune

Auditory discrimination activity

Purpose

Here is another musical game to help your child develop their auditory discrimination and processing skills. The purpose is to help them increase their ability to listen and focus while trying to figure out what song was played.

How to

Play or hum the melody of a song without singing the lyrics and ask your child to "name the tune." This is more challenging for children when they don't have the lyrics to guide them. Playing the melody on an instrument takes some musical skill, but instruments such as the xylophone, piano or recorder are fun to learn for this purpose. For fun, take turns with your child humming melodies and having the listener "name the tune."

Personal reflections

Full disclosure: some children (and adults) get annoyed with me for constantly asking them to "name the tune." My recommendation is to find the right time for this activity when you have a receptive player.

What songs can your child identify from only the melody?

Notes

"Peter and the Wolf"

by Sergei Prokofiev

Auditory discrimination activity

Purpose
Your child will increase their auditory discrimination skills and ability to focus and pay attention through learning to identify a variety of orchestral musical instruments by their sound and melody. In addition, they will learn to match a melody and instrument sound to an animal, use their imaginations and improve their creativity.

How to
Listen to a recording of "Peter and the Wolf" by Sergei Prokofiev with your child. Help them remember which instrument and melody go with which animal. Each time the instrument and melody plays, ask them which animal it represents.

Note: This activity is recommended for children who are aged four to five years old and older due to the concepts of the story. If your child finds the story too scary then put it on a shelf until they are older and more able to enjoy and learn from the story.

7

MANAGING FEELINGS AND DEVELOPING FOCUS THROUGH MUSIC

Managing Anxiety, Anger, Meltdowns, Fear of Trying New Things, Difficulty Focusing and Transitions to New Situations

In my music therapy practice, I get many calls from parents asking for ways to help their young children learn to manage difficult feelings, control challenging behaviors and increase their ability to pay attention and focus. They are concerned when anxiety, fears, anger, meltdowns, difficulty focusing and paying attention, trouble with transitions and resistance to trying new things limit their child's social and educational experiences and negatively affect their family life. While difficult feelings and challenging behaviors are a normal part of growing up, in the extreme they can affect a child's development and a family's harmony.

We want our children to:

- learn to manage frustrating feelings and situations easily

- be able to control their difficult feelings before they turn into a meltdown

- be comfortable and curious, not anxious, such as when going to preschool or on playdates or when staying with a caregiver

- be open to trying new activities and foods

- be able to focus and control their bodies, feelings and minds in order to learn new things

- be able to manage transitions easily and comfortably.

While an inherited temperament, a disability or an experience of trauma, illness or injury can contribute to challenging behaviors, we can still help our children learn to better manage emotional and behavioral difficulties. Children can learn a variety of coping strategies, and we can create environments to help them function to the best of their abilities. Specifically, children can learn ways to feel more confident, soothe themselves, think before acting, challenge negative thought patterns and develop greater empathy for the needs of others.

Music can play an important role in building these skills and abilities. Music matters in learning to manage big feelings, control behavior and developing focus and attention.

The brief overview that follows offers some common-sense strategies for using music to help children build skills in these areas. These suggestions are by no means meant as a "cure" nor as a comprehensive review of strategies. There is no "one-size-fits-all" approach to helping with these issues. Rather, they comprise a starting point to help you, your child and your family use music to better negotiate this often-difficult terrain.

If you have a child with more complicated needs resulting in extreme feelings or behaviors, I encourage you to consult your child's pediatrician or other professional to develop strategies to help your child.

And a reminder, as discussed in Chapter 2, the starting point for helping our young children learn, grow and develop, especially when we are talking about difficult emotions and behaviors, is always a safe, trusting and responsive relationship. When children trust that their needs will be met, they will more likely be able to learn to successfully manage emotional, attentional and behavioral challenges.

Anxiety

Have you ever watched a squirrel? Squirrels often appear anxious, scanning the environment, running this way and that, and then, seemingly out of nowhere, freezing in place. Their vigilance helps them stay alive and avoid predators. The world is not a safe place for squirrels, and they need to be on the constant lookout for danger in order to survive.

For humans, too, anxiety is an adaptive strategy that helps us pay heightened attention to our environment. Fears and anxieties help us mobilize and escape potentially unsafe situations. They can also help us learn which potentially dangerous situations we should avoid in the future. So some level of anxiety can be healthy. But if a child's level of anxiety becomes too intense, interferes with daily activities and prevents them from doing activities that pose no real danger, then we should be ready to help out.

How and when anxiety develops

Anxiety and fears sometimes surface during the toddler and preschool years as imaginations develop and children's minds expand. As they develop the ability to conceptualize things that are not right in front of them, some children imagine bad things and perceive danger in situations that are actually safe (that monster hiding under their bed, or in the closet!).

For some, predisposition towards anxiety or sensitivity to their environment is biological and part of an inherited temperament (Gottschalk and Domschke 2017). For others, fear and anxiety are a response to a scary or traumatic experience. For many, it is a combination of the two factors. A child who has had a scary encounter with a barking or growling dog may develop an overriding fear of all dogs, even the gentlest ones. This kind of overgeneralization can cause problems and restrict children from trying out new experiences that are important for development and learning. If the child who is afraid of dogs avoids going to the playground out of fear that a dog may be there, his experience will sadly be limited. He will miss out on some wonderful play and exercise experiences.

For some children, anxiety and fears affect their comfort to *try new things*. Sometimes children avoid trying new things out of fear of making a mistake. They may be scared that they won't be able to learn the new activity. Sometimes children don't like the feeling of being out of control, and trying something new can feel out of control and unsafe. Some children, however, avoid something new because of a sensory issue—they don't like the texture of a new kind of food, for example, or the lights on an amusement park ride are too bright.

Many children like what they know. They like the comfort and predictability of what's familiar. It helps them feel safe and in control of their environment. They like to practice what they're good at over and over and over again. They like to sing the same songs. It feels good to do what you know how to do.

In music, there is a saying: "Play what you know and practice what you don't know." When we try new things and learn new skills, we can expand our horizons and learn new things that we may actually like and feel good about. This doesn't mean we can't do what we know and love. But rather, by trying new things we can add to our repertoire of things we know and love.

Techniques for managing anxiety

A variety of authors have articulated effective techniques for supporting children in learning to manage and cope with anxiety (Baker 2015; Compton *et al.* 2004; Huebner 2006; Rapee *et al.* 2008). These strategies include:

- teaching children to calm their bodies through relaxation techniques such as deep breathing, meditation and physical exercise

- engaging in distracting activities that are relaxing and fun when children have intrusive anxious thoughts

- challenging the erroneous thought patterns that contribute to anxiety and encouraging new ways of thinking about situations that are based on the actual, rather than imagined, level of danger

- gradual exposure through helping children gradually face a feared object or situation, until they learn there is no real danger.

Using music to reduce anxiety

Music can play a positive role in helping children learn these strategies and better cope with anxious feelings. We can support our children to learn calming musical techniques, including deep breathing to a slow, steady beat, singing gentle, calming songs, listening to relaxation music, as well as distracting from obsessive worry and making up songs to help challenge negative ways of thinking. Physiologically, these techniques can actually lower heart rates and reduce stress levels; emotionally, they can provide a gentle, calming environment within which to confront the causes of their anxiety.

Breathe deeply to a beat

Teach your child how to take long, slow, deep breaths in and out through the nose. Try doing this to a slow, steady beat. The even rhythm helps make sure they are breathing calmly and slowly. It is also relaxing to hear. You can use a metronome (an electronic beat keeper) to maintain the slow pace. (There are many free metronome apps available for smartphones and tablets.) Set your metronome to 60 beats per minute and encourage your child to breathe in for four clicks and out for six clicks. Encourage them to start with taking five deep, slow breaths and then increase to ten as they become more comfortable with the process. You can experiment with the exact number of beats per minute that is comfortable for your child. Using a slow, steady beat to regulate the breaths will help your child to actually slow down and relax. Fast, random and irregular breaths don't work as well. Deep breathing isn't just a trick—it actually provides a physiological benefit in helping us to feel calm (Jerath *et al.* 2006; Russo, Santarelli and O'Rourke 2017).

Encourage your child to practice her "nose breaths" even when she isn't anxious in order for her to learn the technique. Try modeling deep breathing every now and then, in stressful moments, so she can see you do it to help calm yourself as well. Encourage your child to do her "nose breaths" in triggering situations to help prevent her from becoming overly anxious. For example, if preschool is generating anxiety for your child (and perhaps for you as well!), you and your child can take five deep, rhythmic breaths together before entering the school building.

Sing slow songs

When your child is anxious, try singing slow songs together, or sing your favorite songs at a slow speed. We want them to entrain, or join, their rhythms to the slow speed of the song to calm themselves. This may also have the additional effect of distracting them from intrusive anxious thoughts.

You can combine slow songs with deep breathing by encouraging your child to breathe in and out slowly to the beat of the song while they are singing. Some examples of slow songs included in this book that tend to be sung slowly and that are great for this purpose include Twinkle, Twinkle Little Star (Ch. 2), Frère Jacques (Ch. 4) and Hush Little Baby (Ch. 4).

Build a relaxation playlist

Make a playlist of recordings of slow, comforting relaxation music that your child likes. Encourage him to help you pick out some of the songs. As your child develops a relaxing response to these songs over time, just hearing them briefly may help them calm down. Try putting this music on in situations that you know trigger anxiety, before he becomes anxious, as well as when he is feeling anxious. You can include access to this playlist in your "music area" of your house so your child can hopefully learn to listen to it on his own initiative when feeling anxious.

Develop a set of "your songs"

We talked in an earlier chapter about creating a personal library of songs to share with your child that symbolize or represent your relationship with her. These songs can help her out when you're not around. These songs can remind your children of your shared love when they are scared, help them feel safe and protected, and give them strength to calm and soothe themselves. These songs can offer comfort like a teddy bear or security blanket.

When your child is going to be in a potentially anxiety-producing situation—particularly one that involves separation anxiety—remind him that he can sing one of these songs to comfort himself. It can function like a calming mantra, help him build resilience and internalize the strength of his relationship with you. You might also consider giving the lyrics or even a recording of the song to caregivers and preschool teachers to use when your child needs a "soothing moment."

Challenge dysfunctional thoughts with "think like a scientist" songs

Jed Baker, PhD, award-winning author, clinical psychologist, one of my closest childhood friends and, as I mentioned earlier, excellent drummer, explains Cognitive Behavior Therapy to kids as learning to "think like a scientist" in order to reduce anxious thoughts (Baker 2015). Baker asks children two simple questions when they have a worry: "Are you overestimating how likely it is something bad will happen?" and "How bad would it really be if it did happen?" Together, Baker and his clients, like scientists, "research" the evidence that the imagined event could really happen or how bad it would be if it did. This approach will work best with highly verbal children, even as young as three or four, who can comprehend the idea that something is not likely to happen.

For a child who is fearful of riding the bus to school because of worries about traffic accidents, for example, look up the safety data of the bus company. Share that information, along with the safety procedures the company employs to make sure every child is taken care of. (A side benefit of this exercise: It will probably help *you* feel better about sending your child off on that bus as well!)

Music can be a very effective reinforcement of "thinking like a scientist." One can write a song to strengthen thinking about the evidence that shows the child will be safe. In the example above, one could write a little song about bus safety to reinforce the facts. You can sing this song each morning to reassure your child. It doesn't matter how "professional" the song is; it's the repetition of the facts that makes the difference. You can write your own melody or take a familiar song, e.g. "Twinkle, Twinkle Little Star," and write your own "Science Song" lyrics to that melody. This is a method that preschool teachers use all the time!

Here's an example:

The bus drivers are very good
They drive slowly through the neighborhood
They've never lost anyone
They always bring you to your home
The bus drivers are very good
They drive slowly through the neighborhood

The repetition, rhythm, melody and rhyming of songs help engage children and reinforce the learning of information in the lyrics. And remember, from Chapter 1, an added benefit is that singing together can also increase the release of social bonding hormones and reduce the release of stress hormones! Now, I know that school buses sometimes do actually have problems. But the goal is to help children align the level of their fears with the actual probability of danger in a given situation. Try making up your own songs based on your child's individual anxieties and fears.

Encourage spontaneous songs

Encourage your child to make up songs in the moment about his thoughts and feelings whenever he is feeling anxious. Spontaneous singing and songwriting is a great way to work through fears, as well as distract him from his anxious thoughts. And if you can get him to sing the songs for you, you will learn a great deal about what he is feeling and what's on his mind. Get him started by suggesting some initial lyrics to guide him in any situation; for example, start singing "I'm a little scared because…" and let him fill in the rest based on the situation itself. You can also encourage him to spontaneously sing about how he can cope with a feared situation by starting lyrics for him to finish, such as "I can do this because…"

Even at a young age, this strategy can help children learn to process more difficult emotions as well as, as I mentioned above, give you a window into what they're thinking and feeling. I've worked with many young children who, after developing a trusting relationship, have opened up about different fears such as of bees stinging them or going to a new school, or who have used this technique to demonstrate their learning of strategies to cope. For example, the child mentioned above sang about his fears of going to the playground by singing "I'm a little scared because…I'm afraid of bees stinging me." Another child showed their learning by singing, "I can do this because…mistakes are OK because they help you learn." While at first this last child seemed to be parroting my lessons, he was eventually able to engage in trying new and more challenging activities. You can use this strategy to help children learn about many different fears and feelings, including going to school, being left with a caregiver, trying something new, a new (or current) sibling, making friends and having playdates, going on a vacation or any situation in which a child is experiencing difficult feelings.

Use songs and dance to change your mind's channel when obsessively worrying

Help your child use musical strategies to "change their mind's channel" to a less anxious show. Though one may not be able to get rid of the anxious thoughts, by focusing on other productive things, a child can learn to function despite the background noise of anxious thoughts. Through singing and dancing actively, a child can stop focusing on what is causing them anxiety, expel anxious feelings, and calm themselves. This can help him refocus his mind to something less anxiety producing. In addition to distraction from obsessive worry, "changing channels" can empower children and give them the confidence to gradually face previously fearful situations.

When your child is experiencing anxiety, encourage him to dance actively to or sing his favorite song. Your child will eventually learn that through employing simple musical strategies he can change his thought patterns—that they don't have to control him.

One of my favorite dances to help change channels is a "freeze dance." Through the act of focusing on listening for "go" and "stop" and moving one's body actively, children can let go of other, more fearful thoughts. See Chapter 3 for detailed suggestions of ways to do a freeze dance. A terrific children's song, and a good one for distracting children from fears or anxieties, is the "add-on" song "Green Berry Tree." Each time through the song, the singers add an animal and the sound they make to the verse. (This is also a great memory-building song, as children have to remember the ever-lengthening sequence of animals each time through the song.)

"Green Berry Tree"

Traditional

I had a rooster and the rooster pleased me
I fed my rooster from the green berry tree
The little rooster went "cock-a-doodle-do,
De doodlie, doodlie, doodlie do."

[2nd time]
I had a [fill in your animal here] and the [fill in your animal here] pleased me
I fed my [fill in your animal here] from the green berry tree

The little [fill in your animal here] went [fill in your animal's sound here]
The little rooster said "cock-a-doodle-do,
De doodlie, doodlie, doodlie do."

[3rd time]
I had a [fill in your animal here] and the [fill in your animal here] pleased
me
I fed my [fill in your animal here] from the green berry tree
The little [fill in your animal here] went [fill in your animal's sound here]
The little [fill in 2nd animal here] went [fill in 2nd animal's sound here]
The little rooster said "cock-a-doodle-do,
De doodlie, doodlie, doodlie do."

Continue the song by adding new animals along to the verse until you've successfully helped your child let go of some of the intrusive anxious thoughts, and/or you can't remember the ever-lengthening list of animals.

Anger

Anger motivates us to action. Heart rates increase and muscles tense. Anger can propel us to do something to fix a problem, right a wrong, avenge a slight or protect ourselves. Anger is a common human emotion that we all experience at times. Some children are more prone to anger than others due to difficulties that make managing their environment more challenging.

Anger can result from frustration—because a need or want has not been met—or be a sign that a child is in distress. It can be the result of a triggering situation, such as when a toy is taken away or they feel slighted by another child. Children can more easily get angry when they are tired or hungry and have fewer internal resources to manage situations in more constructive ways. Learning challenges, attentional or sensory issues, anxiety, trauma or an underlying disability or disorder can all contribute to greater frustration and anger (Baker 2008).

As with anxiety, children can learn strategies to calm themselves when they are feeling angry. They can learn to manage their thoughts, feelings and bodies to express and communicate their anger in ways that are more constructive and acceptable. Children can learn to understand what triggers their anger and take steps to either avoid or better manage those situations in the future.

Common approaches to helping children manage and cope with anger (e.g. Baker 2008; Matthews 2008) involve helping them learn to:

- take breaks and use relaxation strategies
- identify and alter triggering situations
- constructively communicate anger
- develop the belief that every problem has a solution if one can remain calm
- find ways to more effectively problem solve.

Music can be used effectively to reinforce all of the above techniques to manage anger.

Using music to manage anger

Music can both directly and indirectly alter children's emotions such as anger. It can serve as a distraction and/or relaxation strategy to directly change a mood. Alternatively, music can indirectly impact anger by teaching skills to help children avoid getting angry in the first place when a previous trigger to anger occurs. As you'll see, some of these techniques are similar to managing anxious feelings.

Take musical breaks

When children are starting to feel angry, we can help them learn to take a "musical break" until they calm down and are ready to talk. Have a music "break area" set up in your home or classroom. This can be the same "music area" mentioned throughout the book but with items that help them defuse their angry feelings. Include a music player with relaxation song playlists and some musical instruments. You can model taking a "music break" when you feel angry by sitting in the "break area," putting on some relaxing classical music, closing your eyes and breathing slowly to the beat of the music.

Use relaxation techniques through music

The same relaxation techniques described above for anxiety can be used to help diffuse angry feelings—deep breathing, slow songs, calming playlists, "your" songs, and so on.

Building skills to handle triggers to anger

For many children, challenges such as sharing, taking turns, getting teased, losing a game, making a mistake, struggling with a difficult task or having to wait can trigger anger. There are great musical games that help children build skills to better cope with these triggers. You can coach them during these games to help them focus on the skills they need at that particular moment and positively reinforce them when they begin to practice these behaviors.

For example, for some young children, waiting is very challenging and can trigger angry feelings. Taking turns as a "freeze dance" leader is a great opportunity to help them build skills to both learn how to wait as well as build their tolerance to be able to wait for longer periods. Help them realize that waiting is an opportunity to learn. As they wait for their turn to "start and stop" the music, and start to get angry at not being the leader, encourage them to watch and learn from how others are leading and freezing. Point out the moves people are doing as they freeze, or how the leader is doing short or long periods of dancing in between freezes. Remind them to pay attention to these aspects. Also help them learn that when they wait calmly, they will get a turn. For children who find waiting very challenging, I suggest starting with having them wait to be the leader for short periods at first, maybe have them go second or third, and then building their "waiting period" over time by having them go fourth or fifth.

Use physical activity to express and release anger

Music is a great way for children to release and vent their anger before they are able to talk about and understand why they were angry in the first place.

- **Drumming** allows children to use "big" and "strong" arm motions to release their anger, and then eventually to play more quietly, returning their bodies to a calmer place. You can ask them if they want to play their drum alone while you listen or play together. After your child vents her angry feelings, encourage her to play more and more in control, making music with a steady beat or an interesting rhythm. The goal is to help children regain control of their bodies and minds through more intentional, controlled music-making.

- **Dancing** is another great way for children to use their entire bodies to release difficult feelings like anxiety or anger. Ask your child to dance his feelings. Let him choose the music from a child-friendly playlist that includes both fast and slow songs. The goal is to help him get the anger out of his system so he can begin to understand what triggered it in the first place. Helping children stay "in control" of their bodies, to be safe and not to inflame their anger is an important task for parents and caregivers. If certain songs seem to be having the opposite effect by winding them up even more, try changing to a song with a calmer and more grounding beat.

- In addition to learning how to wait, **go/stop and freeze activities** can also be used to help children learn and practice self-control, both when they are calm and when they are angry. Use recorded music and dancing (such as freeze dances), or play go/stop with musical instruments like maracas, tambourines or drums. By "freezing" their bodies, they are learning a technique for self-control and regulation.

As mentioned previously, for young children, I never use the "you're out if you move after the music stops" rule for freeze dances, as this just adds to the angry feelings. Just encourage your child to freeze when the music stops, and if she doesn't, then remind her to stop, and just keep going with the game without giving it any more attention. If you're playing with more than one child, offer positive reinforcement to children who are "freezing" to encourage the "non-freezing" children to follow the directions.

Meltdowns

The early years are filled with big feelings. Sometimes these big feelings can cause our child's brain to have a "meltdown." Both anger and anxiety can intensify to the point of a meltdown. During meltdowns children become overwhelmed by emotions. Triggers to anger and anxiety, as well as exhaustion or hunger, can contribute to a meltdown.

Jed Baker's useful book *No More Meltdowns* (2008) presents some useful steps for parents who want to help their children cope with meltdowns. These include:

- using humor to distract your child before he or she goes into a meltdown

- learning to de-escalate a meltdown through distraction and soothing techniques

- understanding common triggers to meltdowns

- developing prevention strategies for each of the common triggers to meltdowns prevention include caregivers altering triggering situations and children learning skills to cope with anticipated triggers.

Using music to manage meltdowns

Music offers a variety of opportunities for managing meltdowns by: (1) derailing the meltdown before it starts through humor, (2) calming children (or helping them calm themselves) in the throes of a meltdown, and (3) learning skills to cope better with anticipated triggers.

Distracting through humor

Silly songs can help avert a meltdown before it starts. Sometimes, when given the choice of two paths, a child will take the silly one! Here are a couple of fun songs you can try:

"Apple Tree"

Traditional

Apple tree	
Apple tree	
Will your apple	
fall on me?	
I won't cry	[pretend you are crying]
I won't shout	[sing loudly]
If your apple	
knocks me out	[pretend an apple fell on your head]

"Do Your Ears Hang Low?"

Traditional

Do your ears hang low?	[put each hand upside down next to each ear and wiggle fingers]
Do they wobble to and fro?	
Can you tie them in a knot?	[pretend to tie a knot in a ribbon with both hands in front of you]
Can you tie them in a bow?	
Do you throw them over your shoulders,	[pretend to throw the "knot and bow" over one shoulder]
like a continental soldier?	[salute]
Do your ears hang low?	[put each hand upside down next to each ear and wiggle fingers]

DO YOUR EARS HANG LOW? DO THEY WOB-BLE TO AND FRO? CAN YOU

TIE THEM IN A KNOT CAN YOU TIE THEM IN A BOW? CAN YOU THROW THEM OVER YOUR SHOULDER LIKE A

CON- TIN -EN - TAL SOL - DIER? DO YOUR EARS HANG LOW?

De-escalating through relaxation

Relaxation techniques that are helpful in calming anger and averting anxiety can also be useful in coping with meltdowns. See strategies described previously for deep breathing and musical breaks to help calm the "brain chaos" of a meltdown. You can also hold and rock your child to a steady beat until she is calm and able to begin to understand what triggered their meltdown. Remember to use some of "your songs" from your personal song library during these moments as your child may have visceral associations to them that help her to more easily calm herself.

Practicing skills to manage triggering situations

As described above, you can use music throughout the day to help your child build her social-emotional skills in order to better manage situations that trigger meltdowns, as well as anger and anxiety. Common triggers for meltdowns include trying difficult tasks, waiting for turns, making mistakes, getting teased and difficulty labeling and expressing feelings. Musical activities offer children opportunities to learn and practice skills to manage their difficult feelings before they turn into meltdowns. We can coach them before, during and after situations that commonly trigger them to help them build skills and learn from their experiences.

Trying something difficult

Learning is filled with challenges, and for some children, trying something difficult can trigger anxiety, anger and meltdowns. There are a number of things we can do to help our children learn to manage making mistakes and persevere, and reduce anxiety, anger and meltdowns, as they try difficult tasks, including:

- modeling trying something difficult
- modeling making a mistake, to show it is part of the learning process
- offering them activities or experiences that are slightly more challenging than what they know how to do
- explaining how to do the new task, showing them what needs to be done, and then letting them try on their own
- breaking down a new task into small steps and demonstrate them one at a time, and asking them to try each small step before putting all the steps together
- providing positive reinforcement when they persevere in trying something challenging, including when they make mistakes
- encouraging them to ask for help when they need it.

Using music to learn to try difficult things

Music offers us opportunities to help our children learn to try difficult things. We can model trying to learn new songs, dances and musical instruments and how we cope with making mistakes. Provide slightly more challenging variations on a song and activities that they already know. Break down new songs or dances into small, manageable and easy-to-learn parts, and we can make this a fun activity.

Model learning a new song or music skill
Show your child that it's both fun and challenging to learn something new. If they have a toy instrument—a xylophone or ukulele—try to figure out how to play a new song on it yourself. Or take up learning an instrument yourself, and let your child see how much fun it can be to learn something new and master a new skill. Show them that nobody learns to play an instrument right away, and that practice helps you get better and expand your horizons. Model asking for help when you don't know how to play a chord on your guitar or know the lyrics to a song. Call up a friend, look it up online or ask your child for help in figuring it out.

Model making a mistake

Purposefully make mistakes when singing, dancing or playing an instrument. Laugh it off, try again and then get it right. Or try again and get it wrong, and then ask your child to show you how you're supposed to do it. Show your child that making mistakes is OK, that it's part of the learning process.

Teach slightly more challenging variations of a task they already know

Teach your child a new verse of a song or help them learn how to play the melody on a xylophone or piano, to a song that they already know or are familiar with. I sometimes teach my clients how to play a small part of a song on a xylophone, such as the "E-I-E-I-O" part of "Old MacDonald." We then sing the song and they play that part every time it comes around. The notes for this part in the key of "C" are "E, E, D, D, C." The goal is to challenge them but within reach of what they are capable of learning. The goal is to help them learn how to persevere when they are feeling challenged while also building confidence.

Explain the task

Explain and model to your child how to play an instrument or do a dance. Show them how it's done. Then let them try on their own. Some children benefit from hearing and seeing how to do something, and then having the opportunity to work on it at their own pace. Try not to hover or comment while they are trying it on their own.

Break down the new task into small steps

Teach a new song, dance or game by breaking it into teeny tiny steps. As mentioned previously, I like to teach songs in "echo" form by asking children to first echo one or two words at a time throughout the entire song. Then I have them echo four words, then eight and on and on until they can echo the entire line of the song. Then I ask them to echo two whole lines at a time. Finally, for short songs, I ask them to echo the entire song. Breaking the learning process down into small, manageable pieces can help children feel more comfortable about learning something new.

Transitions

Transitions can sink the best of us, especially when we're in a rush or stressed. Children commonly have difficulty with transitions for several reasons. Sometimes the challenge stems from their not knowing or remembering what to do or what's expected of them during the transition. Other times they don't want to stop what they're currently doing, or they're not thrilled about the next activity. Some children temperamentally are sensitive to change and simply have difficulty switching gears. Sometimes, we adults are so wrapped up in our responsibilities of the transition that we struggle with taking the time to actually help our children prepare for the change. And if we're not calm ourselves, it stresses our children—through our rushing, multi-tasking, being distracted or anticipating our children fighting with each other or us. Take a minute to think about what energy you bring to helping your children get through meals, bedtime and going to daycare or preschool and how it might affect their behavior.

Children are better able to manage transitions if they:

- know what to do and what's expected of them during the transition

- learn the benefits of their next activity

- learn that when they follow directions now they'll have more chance to do what they like later

- feel more in control through knowing the schedule and by being able to predict what's next.

Using music to manage transitions

As is true for many challenging situations, music can help children learn to manage transitions more comfortably and easily. Observe a preschool teacher for a day, and you will most likely hear many transition songs, at the beginning and end of the day, and in between activities. From "hello songs" to "circle time songs" to "cleanup songs," music is used to signal to children that one activity is finishing and another is beginning, to help them learn what to do during the transition, and to help ease the anxiety of changing activities. These types of songs can put them subconsciously into "transition mode."

You can identify songs—perhaps specifically designed for helping children through transitions, or perhaps simply made up spontaneously as new transitions present themselves—and then sing these songs or play recordings of them. Transition songs can help your child become accustomed to specific transitions, and therefore better able to manage them in daily life both with and without music.

Hello and goodbye songs

Hello and goodbye songs help signal the beginning and end of the day or activity. As a music therapist, I start each group I lead at preschools with a hello song and end with a goodbye song. Over time, with repeated exposure to the same hello and goodbye songs, children eventually automatically transition their minds and bodies when they hear the songs. The hello song helps children let go of what they were doing and transition to the activity that I am leading. The goodbye song helps them know that my activity is coming to an end and indicates that something new and different will be starting. Children can prepare to "switch gears" out of music when they hear the goodbye song.

Think of TV theme songs. These are basically hello and goodbye songs. When we hear the theme song of our favorite show, we're primed to be receptive to the show. They help set the stage and prepare us for the characters and story. It puts us in a mood for the show. Sometimes, when I hear the theme song of a show I am currently watching, my mind automatically reminds me of where I'm at in terms of the storyline. When the theme song comes on at the end of the show, it signals to me, often with a little disappointment, that that installment is over and helps me transition out of the show. It helps me refocus my mind to what I need to do next.

You can use specific songs at home to help with beginnings and ends of activities or situations to help manage the "hellos" and "goodbyes." You may want to play a recording or sing a specific song every morning as your children wake up and get ready for their day. Over time, they will most likely associate the song with the morning routine, and these associations can help them know what to do without your having to tell them.

Below is a hello/goodbye song that I wrote and use on a daily basis. I use the same melody and song structure for the hello and goodbye versions of the song, just substituting "goodbye" for "hello." You can also make up your own, or look for hello songs on the internet, or ask your child's preschool teacher, to learn more songs. See Chapter 8 for a variation on this song to learn how to say "hello" in different languages.

"Everybody Shout Hello/Shout Goodbye"

by Jeffrey Friedberg © 2000

Everybody shout hello	*[HELLO!]*
Everybody shout hello	*[HELLO!]*
Everybody shout hello	*[HELLO!]*
Everybody shout hello	*[HELLO!]*
Everybody's dancing round	
Move those feet upon the ground	
Everybody shout hello	*[HELLO!]*
and...	
Everybody shout goodbye	*[GOODBYE!]*
Everybody shout goodbye	*[GOODBYE!]*
Everybody shout goodbye	*[GOODBYE!]*
Everybody shout goodbye	*[GOODBYE!]*
Everybody's dancing round	
Move those feet upon the ground	
Everybody shout goodbye	*[GOODBYE!]*

Variation: Try adding movements instead of "hello" and "goodbye," such as "Everybody...clap your hands" or "Everybody...tap your knees."

Lullabies

Lullabies are basically "goodbye" transition songs, moving children to "bedtime mode" and from being awake to sleeping and to saying "goodbye" for the night. You may want to have a brief running list of specific songs that you sing every night, to help your child manage the transition to bedtime and sleep (see Chapter 4).

In-between transition songs

Transition songs usually motivate children to move and change gears and/or include instructions on the what, where and how of the transition. If you make up your own in-between transition songs, try to include directions that outline the specifics of what your child needs to do, how they should behave, where their materials go and where they should be after they complete these tasks.

For children who are more resistant to change, the lyrics as well as the mood of the music can help motivate them to action and ease anxiety. I love playing the 1980s song "Walking on Sunshine," by Katrina and the Waves, to get my young clients moving during transitions. This song has a fun, upbeat rhythm that reflects the happy lyrics—"I'm walking on sunshine"—both of which help get young feet moving. Of course, you can find more contemporary transition songs if you'd like; this just happens to be a favorite "get going" song from my youth.

Try making a list of specific recorded songs that you play at different times of the day for each transition. Children will eventually associate these songs with specific transitions. Play an upbeat pop song in the morning to get your child energized for the day, a calming song for after daycare or preschool, and a fun dance song for helping to set the table for dinner. And then you can play your lullabies to signal it's time to start bedtime routines. Try to use the same songs for each transition, so your child begins to associate that song with what's expected for that transition.

Transition songs can be popular or children's songs. Come up with your own playlists, but here are some examples of songs you might use during your day to help manage transitions:

- Waking-up energizing song: "La Bamba" as performed by Los Lobos (one of my favorite versions of this song).

- After-school calming song: "This Pretty Planet" by John Forster and Tom Chapin.

- Fun setting the table for dinner song: "Don't Worry, Be Happy" by Bobby McFerrin.

- Getting ready for bedtime song: "What a Wonderful World" as performed by Louis Armstrong.

Write your own transition songs

You can easily make up transition songs that respond to your own child's particular fears or anxieties. For children who are unnerved by having to leave for preschool or daycare, for example, try making up a "Going to School Song" that outlines what is happening and what is expected of them, and that reassures them that they will see you again when the day is done.

Here's an example of a "Going to School Song" that I wrote based on the melody of "Twinkle, Twinkle Little Star":

Now it's time to go to school,
you will learn things that are cool,
afterwards I will give you a hug
and then together we will dance on the...rug
Now it's time to go to school,
you will learn things that are cool...

Your song doesn't have to be a masterpiece (mine certainly isn't!), but just a pure heartfelt expression that conveys important information, helps your child know what's expected, and offers reassurance that you will be together again afterwards. And the ritual of singing it together each morning may help remind your child that he or she does have fun learning things at school!

You can write songs for any transition including going to the supermarket, meal times, or even going to the doctor (though I've never found a song that helps fully prepare them for getting shots!).

For example, as dinner winds down, try making up a song about the expectations for "pre-bedtime":

Dinner is over
Time to put the dishes away...
Dinner is over
Time to put the dishes away...
Everybody pick up something
and put it in the kitchen

Once the table is clean
pick out a book to read!
Dinner is over
Time to put the dishes away…

Or try writing a song about what your child needs to do before bedtime. You can write the song with your child and ask him to tell you the tasks (in order) that he needs to accomplish before going to sleep. Here's an example:

Bedtime, bedtime, it's time for bed
First we brush our teeth and then we brush our head
Read three books and sing a lullaby
Just before we fall asleep it's time to say goodbye…and I love you

Or try writing a transition song to help your child *stop doing something fun* and do something less fun, but that helps them remember that if he easily manages the transition then he can do the fun thing again later, or a different fun thing. Here's an example of a song to help your child manage the transition from watching TV to going food shopping at the supermarket. The song reminds them that if they are a good sport and easily manage the transition then they'll get to watch one more show when they get back (to the tune of "Skip to My Lou"):

Turn off the TV
Turn off the TV
Turn off the TV
It's time to go food shopping

After we come back
And you are a good sport
After we come back
You can watch one more show

Focus and attention

Children need to learn to focus and to pay attention; these skills are critical to their successful development and can be encouraged from the earliest years. While research suggests that difficulty with focus and attention may have some inherited basis (Thapar *et al.* 1999), environmental experiences also play a role. There are many things we can do to help our children increase their ability to focus and pay attention.

For starters, we can help our children get an age-appropriate amount of exercise during the day and sleep at night; as mentioned in Chapter 4, a lack of sleep can mimic attentional challenges that appear similar to ADHD (Martinelli 2019), and exercise can help alleviate ADHD symptoms (Archer and Kostrzewa 2012). Beyond these basics, however, what else can we do to help our children develop these necessary skills? Common approaches include:

- practicing focus and memory tasks

- providing experiences and lessons that are developmentally and individually appropriate

- breaking tasks down into smaller, easier-to-understand units that are within the length of your child's attention span

- knowing when to actively "teach" and when to let your child learn and figure things out for himself

- using relaxation, mindfulness and meditative techniques, such as deep breathing and guided imagery, to quiet your child's mind and body

- reducing the use of electronics and screens and increasing learning that is hands-on and involves movement.

Using music to increase focus and attention

Music provides children with many opportunities to build focus and attention skills. Music offers age-appropriate ways to learn, including multi-sensory and movement experiences. When children are provided with experiences that are meaningful and relevant to them, they are more likely to increase their ability to focus and pay attention.

Music can help children focus through learning to listen more attentively and to better discriminate what they hear. Music can help children increase their memory of specific information, through rhyming and repetition, but also of structures of songs and concepts; this kind of learning both builds the confidence to learn and provides anchors for new information. The more children know, the more easily they can assimilate new information related to and based on what they've learned; and the more easily they assimilate new information, the more likely they are to pay attention when it is offered.

We can help our children increase their focus by breaking down the learning of songs into small, sequential and cumulative parts; children will learn a process that they can apply to learning new information and skills. We can also give children music to calm their minds and bodies, in order to focus better. Music can help children expel excess energy, leading to an increased attention span.

Every child is unique, however, and some aspects of music can be over-stimulating and therefore detrimental to encouraging focus and attention. Pick and choose the musical strategies that work best for your individual child. Here are a few possibilities.

Setting the mood for focus

Play calming music before starting something new. This can help your child relax and calm their minds and be more prepared to focus on the new task. This is both a way to manage the transition and to refocus and recalibrate their minds for "focusing time." It sounds simple but it works. We are basically preparing our child's mind to focus on the new activity or task.

Imitation games

Engage your child in songs and musical games that involve "echoing" short rhythms or melodies. They will increase their abilities to listen, remember and copy the sounds that you initiate. For example, try clapping a short rhythmic pattern of one, two or three claps, and ask your child to echo you. Do this three times in a row, and then ask her to be the leader. You can use a variety of "body percussion" as well by tapping short rhythms on different parts of your body, for example knee, head or chest taps, or stomping your feet in rhythm. You can also use simple percussion instruments, such as tambourines, rhythm sticks or drums.

Encourage your child to imitate your rhythm with the same tempo to help increase recall abilities. As she masters echoing short patterns, increase the length so she has to focus for longer and have more to listen to, remember and copy; increase your pattern to four, five or six notes, and then to seven, eight or nine. Then reverse the game, and have your child be the "leader" while you imitate her rhythms.

Echo and call-and-response songs

Echo songs and call-and-response songs also provide wonderful opportunities to help children increase their ability to listen, focus and pay attention. The format of echo songs necessitates listening to short phrases of words, remembering them, and then reproducing them. In call-and-response songs, instead of reproducing the sound made by the "caller," the "responder" adds a different part. Both of these kinds of songs engage young brains and help them develop the ability to focus, pay attention and respond appropriately.

Echo songs

See Chapter 3 for "Down by the Bay" and "No More Pie."

Call-and-response song

"John the Rabbit"

Traditional

Call	Response
Old John the rabbit	Oh, yes!
Old John the rabbit	Oh, yes!
Had a mighty bad habit	Oh, yes!
Of going to my garden	Oh, yes!
And eating all my peas	Oh, yes!
And cutting down my cabbage	Oh, yes!
He ate tomatoes	Oh, yes!
And sweet potatoes	Oh, yes!
And if I live	Oh, yes!
To see next Fall	Oh, yes!
I won't have	Oh, yes!
A garden at all!	Oh, yes! (or Oh, no!)

OLD JOHN THE RABBIT OH YES OLD JOHN THE RABBIT OH YES HAD A

MIGHTY BAD HABIT OH YES OF GOING IN MY GARDEN OH YES AND EATING ALL MY PEAS OH YES AND

CUTTING DOWN MY CABBAGE OH YES HE ATE TOM - ATOES OH YES AND SWEET POT - ATOES OH YES AND

IF I LIVE OH YES TO SEE NEXT FALL OH YES I WO - N'T HAVE OH YES A

GARD - EN AT ALL OH YES

Memorizing song lyrics and melodies

Memorizing songs helps children increase their abilities to focus, pay attention and remember—and also their confidence in their ability to learn. Memorizing is a skill. The more songs a child learns, the easier it becomes to learn new songs. The more they know, the more "anchors" they have on which to hang new information, skills and concepts. As they learn one song structure, they can compare new songs to it. All this makes the learning process easier for them and helps them focus and attend. And they are learning that they are capable learners, which can help them to be more eager to learn more. Children focus better when they feel good about their capabilities and want to learn something. And learning songs provides added benefits: an enlarged vocabulary; and an expanded grasp of information and knowledge of concepts.

Encouraging structured and unstructured musical play

Remember that at the very beginning of this book we talked about the *process* of music as opposed to the product? We used Small's word "musick" as a verb. You can help your child develop focus by emphasizing the process of music-making rather than the actual sounds that are produced. Children are more engaged—and therefore more focused—when they are having fun, as opposed to trying to make perfect music.

Children are most successful, learn best and have greater focus when they are learning as they are meant to learn, through using their senses, moving and playing. In the early years, you'll most likely find that children can play for hours but sit and listen to us talk for only minutes. Play is how they are built to learn and focus best.

Managing stimulation

For children who have difficulty with focus and attention, managing the level of stimulation in their immediate environment may be necessary. This includes knowing when to put on relaxing music, when to put on upbeat dance music, and when to turn the music off altogether! For some children, fast music helps energize and focus them; for others, it is extremely distracting. Know your child and what best helps them focus.

Putting it all together

Music is a wonderful tool to help children learn strategies to control their bodies, feelings and minds—all of which helps them manage difficult feelings of anxiety and anger, as well as enhancing their ability to pay attention and focus appropriately, try new things and manage meltdowns and transitions more easily. Relaxation playlists, deep breathing techniques and a variety of musical games and activities can help children learn to soothe themselves at times of stress or intense emotional reactions.

8

DIVERSITY THROUGH MUSIC

Learning to Appreciate Similarities and Differences in Cultures

> *Note:* In this chapter, when referring to culture and diversity, I am writing in a broader sense to include the many different ways children learn to identify themselves and others, including by family, ethnicity, national origin, religion, race, gender, language, abilities and special needs, and physical qualities, to name a few.

As children grow, the network of relationships that influences their development expands from their initial attachments to their family and friends, to school and to their community. These days, mass media also plays an increasingly powerful role in affecting children during early childhood! The impact of these relationships on their developing sense of who they are, who is like them and who is different increases. Culture matters.

The early years are filled with learning the sounds of their native language and the smells and tastes of their food. They learn the way people dress, the different physical characteristics of the people they come in contact with, ways of relating and what is valued, the roles different people play, and the rituals and customs that are observed. The drive to connect with this growing network includes absorbing and developing attitudes towards all of these qualities as they form their cultural identity.

Music is one important way that children learn about and build their cultural identity. Music is also a valuable way that children can learn to appreciate and value—rather than fear—cultures different from their own. We can help our children learn to appreciate their cultures and to view their similarities and differences as just similarities and differences—rather than as greater or less than. Through music, we can also create inclusive environments in which all children have the opportunity to learn and grow to the best of their abilities.

Experience matters in developing cultural attitudes

Our children's attitudes towards cultures matter. How young children view others who are similar to and different from them affects how they think, feel and behave. It affects how children feel about themselves, whether they feel accepted and valued and how well they play, work and learn together.

Children begin to notice differences early. They learn who looks, sounds and behaves like them and differently from them. Infants notice racial differences as early as three months (Kelly *et al.* 2005). Starting around three years old, children begin to develop attitudes towards the qualities of the people around them, including race, gender and abilities (Mac Naughton 2006).

Experiences affect what cultural attitudes children develop. Experiences affect how they feel about and interact with people with qualities similar to and different from their own. According to Hirschfeld (2008), children learn from the example we set at home, but they are also strongly influenced by what they see and hear outside of their family. From family to friends to school to mass media, children pick up cues about the qualities that are valued. For example, they notice the different roles that men and women occupy, how children of different abilities and needs are treated, how different ethnicities are characterized, and how different races are treated and portrayed.

Interculturalism

I find "interculturalism" (Ponciano and Shabazian 2012) to be a powerful approach both for helping us understand the development of cultural identities and for helping children learn about their cultures, share their experiences and develop understanding and appreciation for others different from them. Within this framework, culture is not viewed as a finite, unchangeable set of qualities, and a person is not viewed as being a representative of that culture. Instead, each child is thought of as growing up in a *cultural context*.

A child's cultural context represents his "unique and individual experience" in terms of "ethnicity and race, primary language, family composition, socioeconomic status, and special needs" (Ponciano and Shabazian 2012, p.23). A person is not her culture, and a culture is not monolithic, permanent or stable. Individuals are influenced by their cultures and, in turn, influence and affect it. I think this takes the pressure off each of us to not have to "be our culture," acknowledges that there are many differences within cultures as well as between cultures, and accepts that cultures are in a constant state of change.

In many ways, music reflects this perspective. Even though musicians may play particular "styles" of music, they are individually influenced by what they hear, and in turn influence others. Individual musicians have historically shared and learned within and across cultures, styles and genres. They learn different songs and ways of playing from each other and develop new ways of playing from these combinations. As a result, musical styles, or cultures, are always in a state of change. This aspect of musicians constantly being influenced by and influencing others, within and across styles and cultures, and of musical styles constantly changing and evolving due to the contributions by many individuals, is an important element of what's kept music interesting and relevant. It's also a living reflection of the ever-changing nature of culture. Music reflects both each musician's individual musical cultural context and his or her personal experience within a broader culture.

In interculturalism, culture is not thought of as a top-down curriculum to be taught. Children and adults can learn from each other about each individual's cultural experience. Rather than being taught as if there are different "teams," and that we each play on one of those, children can be taught that we each have different qualities and experiences that inform who we are. Children can learn to both value the qualities of their individual cultural contexts and cultural experiences and be open to learning from the qualities and experiences of others.

We live in a diverse world—both within each culture and between cultures. It is important to help our children learn to appreciate their family and community's culture—the traditions and history, the language and food, the customs and rituals, and the values. It is also important, starting in the early years, to help all of our children feel valued and important members of their community through having their ever-changing and evolving cultural contexts validated as well.

Teaching diversity

As the important adults in our children's lives, we can help them both to manage the influences on their developing cultural context and to understand and confront any biases they may have picked up. Exposure alone is not enough, however, to assist them in deciphering and making sense of what they are learning. We also need to actively teach them (Mac Naughton 2006).

Winkler (2009) writes about five ways of actively helping preschool-age children understand and process questions about race and issues of racial bias. I find these also to be helpful in facilitating understanding of a variety of differences children may notice and have questions about, in addition to race.

- "Talk About It"—have open and frank discussions with children when they notice differences.

- "Be Accurate and Age-Appropriate"—provide accurate responses in ways children can understand.

- "Take It Seriously"—listen for opportunities to discuss racial questions and attitudes.

- "Encourage Complex Thinking"—help children think about multiple ways that people are similar and different at the same time.

- "Empower"—expose children to people who are actively involved in change towards equality and diversity.

Basically, Winkler acknowledges that experiences of actively and directly engaging children around issues of diversity matter to young children in terms of their developing the ability to understand and appreciate our similarities and differences. Experiences are more powerful when we consciously listen for our children's developing attitudes and openly discuss them. Young children are capable of learning from direct age-appropriate conversations about culture. This includes your being open to talking about the observations your child makes about race, religion, gender, nationality, ethnicity, socioeconomic status and/or abilities in a nonjudgmental manner. And children often notice inequity and voice concerns about inequality more openly and directly than adults. It's up to us to listen to, and talk to them frankly about, these issues, and to be open to confronting our own potential biases.

In terms of my experiences, this book, no doubt, has some biases reflecting my cultural context. For example, in terms of sleep hygiene, some cultures may have different values regarding how much sleep is necessary or what age is appropriate for a child to independently soothe themselves to sleep. Some may feel that the "family bed" is important throughout the early years and that it is optimal to wait until children are older to sleep on their own. While the research I quote shows that children have better quantity and quality of sleep through other methods, the value to an individual and her family, due to the cultural context, may outweigh this in the long term.

The viewpoint I present here reflects my interpretation of the scientific research and is informed by my cultural context as well as by the data. I accept and try to be as open as I can to learning how my experiences inform my ideas, both in terms of potential biases and otherwise. Parenting is probably the most influential time for teaching and learning about one's culture. There are many factors that go into our parenting decisions. Especially for our children's sake, it is important for us to be open to both celebrating our culture and confronting cultural biases when they arise.

Music and diversity

Music is a powerful transmitter of culture and also a way that we can help our children share and learn about each other's cultural contexts. From the beginning, we acculturate our children through music. From Day One and even before, as we learned, music influences a child's development from infant directed singing to lullaby and play songs to songs that teach information and build skills. Through music, children are learning the sounds of their language, ways of relating and interacting, the roles different people occupy, what is important to learn, and the skills that are deemed necessary to build.

As they grow, children learn about their families, friends and communities and the different people that occupy them through songs. Families have their sets of songs; preschool is filled with songs to teach and to help manage behavior; countries have their anthems; and religious rituals are filled with songs to help celebrate holidays and mark occasions. You might be surprised, if you really think about it, how much music children hear every day through mass media. Music constantly shapes our experiences, providing a soundtrack to most occasions, from what we play at home to stores and the mall to the supermarket to the elevator to the doctor's office to TV and movies to when we're in the car to celebrations to school. These sounds don't just "go in one ear and out the other." Children's attitudes are being influenced by the music as well as by its social significance.

Using music to build understanding and awareness

The pervasiveness and power of music make it a natural for influencing a child's broader cultural identity or context. It makes sense that we actively use music to build awareness, appreciation and understanding of our cultural similarities and differences.

We can use:

- songs to teach children about their personal cultural backgrounds

- music to help them learn about other people's varied cultural contexts

- music to generate discussions about similarities and differences

- music to build inclusive environments where similarities and differences are viewed as qualities to learn about each other, rather than as being "less or greater than"

- music to build children's thinking skills so they can hold different ideas and feelings at the same time.

Celebrating your own culture through song sharing

Your family's cultural identity can be validated through the sharing of their songs. Celebrate your family's culture by building a playlist of your family's music. Listen to and sing songs that reflect your individual family's preferences as well as your nationality, ethnicity, religion and language.

Exploring other cultures through music

Learn about different cultures by exploring a wide range of music from a wide variety of music-makers. Listen to music, watch videos of musicians, go to concerts and sing songs from different cultures with your child. Make an active effort for your child to see, hear, feel and experience music that reflects different cultural contexts. Children can listen to recordings of songs in different languages and realize that, while the words, rhythms and instruments may be different, it's still "music" and, more often than not, still a lot of fun. Children can engage in play songs from around the world and build symbolic bridges with children from other cultures by learning that they share many of the same qualities.

Generating discussion about differences through music

There are many great songs that help children explore cultural diversity. Share some of these songs and talk about them with your child in an age-appropriate manner. Listen for how your child reacts to what he experiences. Help her to develop language to talk about the similarities and differences she experiences in the music she hears. You can use these songs both to validate your child's family experience and to show that other children have different experiences.

She may notice different instruments, sounds, languages, ways of interacting while making music, roles that men and women play in the music-making, ways of moving to music, ways the musicians dress, and physical differences of the musicians. Each of these qualities can each be a springboard for discussion about different cultural contexts and their similarities and differences.

Building inclusive environments through music

Create inclusive musical environments where all children have opportunities to be successful. Help children learn to value a wide range of qualities, skills and abilities. Find ways to include children of all abilities, races, ethnicities, languages and genders in your music-making. This may mean making an extra effort to choose songs and music as well as early childhood music classes, daycares or preschools that are more inclusive and diverse.

Create musical play environments in which all participants feel valued. Help your children learn that all children are important. Model how to include others who have qualities different from their own.

Sing songs and play music that represents many cultural contexts. Include songs in different languages, from different ethnicities, nations and religions, that help celebrate different cultures' rituals, and that allow for children with different abilities to participate actively. Adapt activities and instruments to meet the needs of all of your children. With groups of children from beyond your own family—at a birthday party, for example—use the songs as opportunities to talk about each child's cultural contexts, similarities and differences, and, when appropriate, their thoughts and feelings about these.

Notice and reinforce all children's participation during activities. Remember that music is a process and not a product. If your children can only sing one word or make one sound of a song, or do one movement of a fingerplay, give them positive reinforcement for this. Validate how much, not how little, your child can do.

Encouraging critical thinking through music

Music can push children to think critically about the world around them and the roles other people play in it. Through music listening and playing, explore, challenge and help change attitudes that children may have developed. For example, sharing music videos of women conducting orchestras may change views about gender roles and who gets to do what job. You can then encourage your daughter or son to explore these roles through having them conduct their own pretend orchestra at home (either to a recording or having you play your tambourine according to their directions!).

Children can make connections with and learn to challenge stereotypes and biases through intimate musical interactions with children with different cultural contexts. When children make music together, and build social bonds through their music, AKA make friends, they get to know the person behind the cultural label.

Children can also learn to hold multiple and sometimes conflicting thoughts and feelings about the music they hear and make. We can help them expand their thinking skills by identifying things they like and don't like, or similarities and differences, within a single piece of music. For example, by asking questions that help them analyze what they are hearing, we can help them articulate that they like the drum beat of a particular song but not the lyrics. Or, from singing together, children can learn that while each child's voice sounds different, when many different voices come together, it can make a new and beautiful sound.

SONGS, GAMES AND ACTIVITIES FOR BUILDING DIVERSITY THROUGH MUSIC

This section includes specific songs and musical activities that you can use to support your children in developing their ability to appreciate diversity. The accompanying music and video files can be downloaded from www.jkp.com/voucher using the code BOOMESE.

The songs I have chosen here are by no means comprehensive or meant to reflect any intention that these cultures should be focused on first, or to the exclusion of others. I chose these simply because I know and like them. And I feel that children respond well to them. *Please* continue your exploration of songs that reflect a wide variety of experiences in terms of nationality, ethnicity, gender, language and ability and any other qualities that you deem relevant to your child's developing cultural identity and context.

"Everybody Shout Hola"

Variation of "Everybody Shout Hello" from Chapter 7

by Jeffrey Friedberg © 2019

Purpose

"Everybody Shout Hola" helps children hear and learn how to say "hello" in different languages. They learn that while languages may sound differently from one another, they have many similarities in what they express—in this case a greeting.

How to

Sing the song one time through shouting "hello" in English. Then ask children for examples of ways to say hello in different languages. If they have difficulty coming up with examples, give them some examples. Try to get or give five examples and sing the song again, but this time plug in their other languages into the "hello" slot. You can use the different languages as a starting point to a discussion of your family's cultural background as well as of a general discussion about different cultures.

Everybody shout hello	[HELLO!]
Everybody shout hello	[HELLO!]
Everybody shout hello	[HELLO!]

Everybody's dancing round	
Put your feet upon the ground	
Everybody shout hello	[HELLO!]
[Ask for examples of how to say "hello" in other languages]	
and…	
Everybody shout hola	[HOLA!]
Everybody shout bonjour	[BONJOUR!]
Everybody shout shalom	[SHALOM!]
Everybody shout Nǐ hǎo	[NǏ HǍO!]
Everybody's dancing round	
Put your feet upon the ground	
Everybody shout ciao	[CIAO!]

Personal reflections

As with most songs, games and activities in this book, you can adapt this to help with many different areas of development. This song is particularly versatile.

In what other languages does your child know how to say hello?

Notes

"Aiken Drum"

Traditional (Scotland)

Purpose

In this traditional Scottish children's song, children learn about names that are different from what they are used to hearing by learning about a character named "Aiken Drum." They can use this lesson as a starting point to learn to be more accepting of others who have different characteristics from them. In addition, they also learn to name different parts of their bodies as they point to the part of the body sung about and use their imagination to come up with a food that resembles it.

How to

Sing the first verse and chorus and ask your child to sing along and clap their hands. For each verse (body part section), ask them to point to the part sung about and try to come up with a food that resembles that part of their body. If they have difficulty coming up with an idea, give them two choices to pick from. Sing the chorus in between each verse and at the end.

There was a man lived in the moon
In the moon
In the moon
There was a man lived in the moon
And his name was Aiken Drum

(Chorus)
And he played on a ladle
A ladle, a ladle
He played on a ladle
And his name was Aiken Drum

(Verse)
His hair was made of _____

_____,' _____
His hair was made of _____
And his name was Aiken Drum

(Chorus)

(Verse)
His ears were made of _____

_____,' _____
His ears were made of _____
And his name was Aiken Drum

(Chorus)

(Verse)
His nose was made of _____

_____, _____
His nose was made of _____
And his name was Aiken Drum_

(Chorus)

Note: You can sing about any part of the body that you'd like to help your child learn the name and identify.

What foods do your children like to pair with parts of their faces?

Notes

"Los Pollitos"

Traditional (Latin America)

I have seen this song described as a popular "Latin American" children's song as well as being attributed to a variety of different countries. With that said, I am not sure of its country of origin.

Purpose

Your child will hear the sounds of the Spanish language and learn the word for baby chicken (pollito) in Spanish. Many children feel pride in mastering words from languages different from their own.

How to

Teach your children that "pollito" is Spanish for baby chicken, or chick. Tell them that in this song the baby chickens sing "pío, pío, pío" when they're tired and hungry; and then their mothers get them corn and wheat to eat; and then they go to sleep under their mother's wing. Slowly sing or play a recording of the song and ask them to sing along.

> Los pollitos dicen
> pío, pío, pío,
> cuando tienen hambrey
> cuando tienen frío.
> La gallina busca
> el maíz y el trigo,
> les da la comida y
> les presta abrigo.
>
> Bajo de sus alas,
> acurrucaditos.
> Duermen los pollitos
> hasta el otro día!

Los Pol - Li - Tos Di - Cen Pi - o Pi - o

Pi - o Cuan - do Tien - en Ham - bre y

Cuan - do Tien - en Fri - o.

How was your "Los Pollitos" experience?

Notes

"Fanga Alafia"

Traditional (Nigeria)

Purpose

Your child will hear the Yoruba language as they learn this Nigerian welcome song. Use this song as an opportunity to talk about the country Nigeria and different ways to say hello and greet people.

How to

I like to teach this song in "echo." Sing the first line and ask your child to echo you. Repeat the process with the second line. After the child masters each line, sing the entire song and ask him to echo you.

Note: I have seen this song referred to as "Fanga Alafia" and "Funga Alafia."

Fanga alafia,
ashe, ashe (repeat)

👍 Personal reflections

People have come up with fun movements and choreography to "Fanga Alafia" that you can find online.

What movements do you like to use when singing "Fanga Alafia"?

Notes

"Rattlin' Bog"

Traditional (Ireland)

Purpose

In this popular Irish "add-on" or cumulative song, children learn a sequence of items that are in the bog. The items progressively go from big to smaller. They will also increase their memory skills in the process!

How to

Sing the song slowly at first, helping the children learn the words from listening as you sing. As they master the lyrics of the chorus and begin to memorize the items in the bog, speed up. As they master the entire song, slow down or pause each time you get to a new item and ask them to fill it in.

Chorus:
Oh ro the rattlin' bog
The bog down in the valley-oh
Oh ro the rattlin' bog
The bog down in the valley-oh

And in the bog,
There was a tree,
A rare tree,
A rattlin' tree,
And the tree in the bog,
And the bog down in the valley-oh!

[Chorus]

And on the tree,
There was a limb,
A rare limb,
A rattlin' limb,
And the limb on the tree,
And the tree in the bog,
And the bog down in the valley-oh!

[Chorus]

And on the limb,
There was a branch,
A rare branch,
A rattlin' branch,
And the branch on the limb,
And the limb on the tree,
And the tree in the bog,
And the bog down in the valley-oh!

[Chorus]

On this branch,
There was a twig,
A rare twig,
A rattlin' twig,
And the twig on the branch
And the branch on the limb,
And the limb on the tree,
And the tree in the bog,
And the bog down in the valley-oh!

[Chorus]

On this twig,
There was a nest,
A rare nest,
A rattlin' nest,
And the nest on the twig,
And the twig on the branch,
And the branch on the limb,
And the limb on the tree,
And the tree in the bog,
And the bog down in the valley-oh!

Note: I have seen different versions with slightly different items, but these are the most common additional things to add at this point: egg, bird, feather and flea.

How was your "Rattlin' Bog" experience?

Notes

"Alle Meine Entchen"

Traditional (Germany)

Purpose

Explore German culture and how languages have different sounds and words for the same object by singing this German children's song about ducks.

How to

Sing and/or listen to recordings of this song in German and English with your child. Discuss the different sounds and words your child hears in the song compared with her native language. Compare the words "duckling" in English and "Entchen" in German. Use this song as a starting point to learn about Germany.

Alle meine Entchen
Schwimmen auf dem See,
Schwimmen auf dem See,
Köpfchen in das Wasser,
Schwänzchen in die Höh.

All my little ducklings,
swimming in the lake,
swimming in the lake.
Their heads in the water,
and tails high in the air.

"Birch Tree"

Traditional (Russia)

Purpose

This Russian folk song is a great way to explore how symbols mean different things to different cultures. You can use the symbol of the "birch tree" as important to the Russian culture as a way to talk about things that are important in your children's culture. "Birch Tree" also helps children hear and learn about a minor musical harmony, which is much different from most children's songs which tend to be in major keys.

How to

Sing and/or listen to recordings of this song with your child. Ask them how it sounds similar and different from other songs they know. Teach them that in the Russian culture the birch tree is thought to be very special and have special powers to keep people safe. They value things made of birch trees. Ask them what things in their culture are thought to be special and help keep them safe.

See the lovely birch in the meadow,
Curly leaves all dancing when the wind blows.
Loo-lee-loo, when the wind blows,
Loo-lee-loo, when the wind blows.

What are your children's or students' favorite trees?

Notes

_____

"Che Che Koolay"

Traditional (Ghana)

Purpose

In this echo song from Ghana, children will learn to make sounds that are most likely different from what they are used to. You can use this song to encourage discussion about similarities and differences of people around the world. Try to focus on how children in different parts of the world may speak different languages but they share a love of singing, dancing and playing. You can further your exploration by looking at photos and videos of children from Ghana to encourage further discussion.

How to

You, or an assigned leader, sing the part on the left and the group echoes it.

Note: I have written the words below in phonetic spelling to help with pronunciation. As far as I can tell from my research, these are sounds and not words.

Leader	Echoer
Chay Chay Koolay	Chay Chay Koolay
Chay Chay Kofisa	Chay Chay Kofisa
Kofisa Langa	Kofisa Langa
Kaka Shay-langa	Kaka Shay-langa
Kum Ay-denday	Kum Ay-denday

Describe your "Che Che Koolay" experience.

Notes

For other songs throughout this book that help children learn about other countries, languages and customs, please see:

A Ram Sam Sam, Morocco (Ch. 5)

Brother, Sister, Dance with Me, Germany (Ch. 3)

Frère Jacques, France (Ch. 4)

Nabe, Nabe, Soku Nuke, Japan (Ch. 3)

Noble Duke of York, England (Ch. 5)

Obwisana, Ghana (Ch. 3).

Conclusion

Are You Ready to Musically Parent?

So, are you ready to try some musical parenting?

Are you ready to use music to bond with your child and help him manage his sleep? Have you tried any of the songs or activities to help your child make friends and have better playdates or to build her physical skills? What's keeping you from using music to help her learn about numbers, letters and colors, to develop confidence in his ability to learn new things and increase his vocabulary and language skills? Any thoughts about using music to manage those big feelings and transitions? What about to build an appreciation of diversity?

As you've read, whether you're raising children, teaching in a classroom or providing therapy or caregiving for a child, music matters and can help. Music is quite versatile and effective. Children can learn across multiple areas of development simultaneously when "musicking." And it's "baked into the cake." As I mentioned in Chapter 1, you've already got the "musical brain," so there's not much you need to do to prepare. You'll basically just be tapping into a process that humans have evolved for thousands of years for our overall health and wellbeing.

I know that, for some, singing and dancing can feel inhibiting, and for others it comes more naturally. But "musicking" with children (and adults) is well worth the effort. And once you get started and see how helpful and fun it can be, it will feel quite effortless, and actually quite joyful.

If you're having trouble getting started, begin slowly and try one song or activity to help with a specific area, such as sleep or playdates. Build a bedtime routine with specific songs that helps your child progressively calm her body, mind and feelings. Or teach him songs that he can use on playdates to learn to work together and take turns. Remember that the goal of musical parenting is to focus on the process of music. It's not to make your child into a professional virtuosic musician. It's not to raise his SAT score or get her into the "right" school. The goal is to help your child use music to learn, communicate, cope, connect and, hopefully, lead a more meaningful and fulfilling life.

I believe that music is essential for healthy development. It shouldn't be considered an option or an extracurricular add-on. I know I may be biased in this regard, but, based on the evidence, I firmly believe that music is one of the most powerful ways for children to engage in the world. Without music we miss out on a uniquely human experience. And the time you spend together and the relationships you form through "musicking" will be filled with big feelings, movement and love.

So, all the best as you go forth and "musically parent."

Jeffrey

References

Ackerman, S. (1992) *Discovering the Brain.* Washington, DC: National Academies Press.

Adam, K. (1980) 'Sleep as a Restorative Process and a Theory to Explain Why.' In P.S. McConnell, G.J. Boer, H.J. Romijn, N.E. Van De Poll and M.A. Corner (eds) *Progress in Brain Research Volume 53,* 289–305. New York: Elsevier.

Allen, S.L., Howlett, M.D., Coulombe, J.A. and Corkum, P.V. (2016) 'ABCs of sleeping: A review of the evidence behind pediatric sleep recommendations.' *Sleep Medicine Reviews 29,* 1–14.

American Academy of Pediatrics (2003) 'Encourage your child to be physically active.' Accessed on 12/23/18 at www.healthychildren.org/English/healthy-living/fitness/Pages/Encouraging-Your-Child-to-be-Physically-Active.aspx.

Archer, T. and Kostrzewa, R.M. (2012) 'Physical exercise alleviates ADHD symptoms: Regional deficits and development trajectory.' *Neurotoxicity Research 212,* 195–209.

Baker, J. (2008) *No More Meltdowns.* Arlington, TX: Future Horizons, Inc.

Baker, J. (2015) *Overcoming Anxiety.* Arlington, TX: Future Horizons, Inc.

Bathory, E. and Tomopoulos, S. (2017) 'Sleep regulation, physiology and development, sleep duration and patterns, and sleep hygiene in infants, toddlers, and preschool-age children.' *Current Problems in Pediatric and Adolescent Health Care 47,* 2, 29–42.

Bowlby, J. (1969) *Attachment and Loss.* New York: Basic Books.

Center on the Developing Child at Harvard University (2018) 'Brain architecture.' Accessed on 12/21/18 at https://developingchild.harvard.edu/science/key-concepts/brain-architecture.

Compton, S.N., March, J.S., Brent, D., Albano, A.M., Weersing, V.R. and Curry, J. (2004) 'Cognitive-behavioral psychotherapy for anxiety and depressive disorders in children and adolescents: An evidence-based medicine review.' *Journal of the American Academy of Child and Adolescent Psychiatry 43,* 8, 930–959.

Corbeil, M., Trehub, S.E. and Peretz, I. (2016) 'Singing delays the onset of infant distress.' *Infancy 21,* 373–391.

Cramer, S.C., Sur, M., Dobkin, B.H. *et al.* (2011) 'Harnessing neuroplasticity for clinical applications.' *Brain 134,* 6, 1, 1591–1609.

Dahl, R.E. (2007) 'Sleep and the developing brain.' *Sleep 30,* 9, 1079–1080.

de l'Etoile, S.K. (2006) 'Infant-directed singing: A theory for clinical intervention.' *Music Therapy Perspectives 24,* 1, 22–29.

Dekaban, A.S. and Sadowsky, D. (1978) 'Changes in brain weights during the span of human life: Relation of brain weights to body heights and body weights.' *Annals of Neurology: Official Journal of the American Neurological Association and the Child Neurology Society 4,* 4, 345–356.

Dionne, G., Touchette, E., Forget-Dubois, N., Petit, D., Tremblay, R.E., Montplaisir, J.Y. and Boivin, M. (2011) 'Associations between sleep-wake consolidation and language development in early childhood: A longitudinal twin study.' *Sleep 34,* 8, 987–995.

Edison Research (2014) 'Edison Research conducts first ever share of ear* measurement for all forms of online and offline audio.' Accessed on 8/1/18 at www.edisonresearch.com/edison-research-conducts-first-ever-share-of-ear-measurement-for-all-forms-of-online-and-offline-audio.

Farrell, A.K., Simpson, J.A., Carlson, E.A., Englund, M.M. and Sung, S. (2016) 'The impact of stress at different life stages on physical health and the buffering effects of maternal sensitivity.' *Health Psychology: Official Journal of the Division of Health Psychology: American Psychological Association 36,* 1, 35–44.

Feierabend, J.M. (2006) *First Steps in Music for Preschool and Beyond.* Chicago, IL: GIA Publications, Inc.

Gabbard, C. and Rodrigues, L. (2007) 'Optimizing early brain and motor development through movement.' *Excelligence Learning Corporation.* Accessed on 12/21/18 at www.earlychildhoodnews.com/earlychildhood/article_print.aspx?ArticleId=360.

Geist, E. (2018) 'Support math readiness through music.' *NAEYC: Our Work / For Families / Articles for Families on Creative Arts and Music / Support Math Readiness Through Music.* Accessed on 11/1/18 at www.naeyc.org/our-work/families/support-math-readiness-through-music.

Gottschalk, M.G. and Domschke, K. (2017) 'Genetics of generalized anxiety disorder and related traits.' *Dialogues in Clinical Neuroscience 19*, 2, 159–168.

Hagan, J.F., Shaw, J.S. and Duncan, P.M. (eds) (2008) *Bright Futures: Guidelines for Health Supervision of Infants, Children, and Adolescents, Third Edition.* Elk Grove Village, IL: American Academy of Pediatrics. Accessed on 10/10/18 at https://brightfutures.aap.org/Bright%20Futures%20Documents/BF4_Introduction.pdf.

Hirschfeld, L.A. (2008) 'Children's Developing Conceptions of Race.' In S.M. Quintana and C. McKown (eds) *Handbook of Race, Racism, and the Developing Child.* Hoboken, NJ: John Wiley & Sons.

Hirshkowitz, M., Whiton, K., Albert, S.M. *et al.* (2015) 'National Sleep Foundation's sleep time duration recommendations: Methodology and results summary.' *Sleep Health: Journal of the National Sleep Foundation 1*, 1, 40–43.

Huebner, D. (2006) *What to Do When You Worry Too Much.* Washington, DC: Magination Press.

Huron, D. (2003) 'Is Music an Evolutionary Adaptation?' In I. Peretz and R. Zatorre (eds) *The Cognitive Neuroscience of Music.* New York: Oxford University Press.

Hyde, K.L., Lerch, J., Norton, A., Forgeard, M., Winner, E., Evans, A. and Schlaug, G. (2009) 'The effects of musical training on structural brain development: A longitudinal study.' *Annals of the New York Academy of Sciences 1169*, 182–186.

Jerath, R., Edry, J.W., Barnes, V.A. and Jerath, V. (2006) 'Physiology of long pranayamic breathing: Neural respiratory elements may provide a mechanism that explains how slow deep breathing shifts the autonomic nervous system.' *Medical Hypotheses 67*, 3, 566–571.

Jones, D.E., Greenberg, M. and Crowley, M. (2015) 'Early social-emotional functioning and public health: The relationship between kindergarten social competence and future wellness.' *American Journal of Public Health 105*, 11, 2283–2290.

Keeler, J.R., Roth, E.A., Neuser, B.L., Spitsbergen, J.M., Waters, D.J.M. and Vianney, J.M. (2015) 'The neurochemistry and social flow of singing: Bonding and oxytocin.' *Frontiers in Human Neuroscience 9*, 518, 1–10.

Kelly, D.J., Quinn, P.C., Slater, A.M. *et al.* (2005) 'Three-month-olds, but not newborns, prefer own-race faces.' *Developmental Science 8*, 6, F31–F36.

Kirschner, S. and Tomasello, M. (2010) 'Joint music making promotes prosocial behavior in 4-year-old children.' *Evolution and Human Behavior 31*, 5, 354–364.

Kisilevsky, B.S., Hains, S.M.J., Lee, K. *et al.* (2003) 'Effects of experience on fetal voice recognition.' *Psychological Science 14*, 3, 220–224.

Kohl III, H.W. and Cook, H.E. (eds) (2013) *Educating the Student Body: Taking Physical Activity and Physical Education to School.* Washington, DC: The National Academies Press.

Kreutz, G. (2014) 'Singing and social bonding introduction.' *Music and Medicine 6*, 2, 51–60.

Lemola, S., Räikkönen, K., Scheier, M.F. *et al.* (2011) 'Sleep quantity, quality and optimism in children.' *Journal of Sleep Research 20*, 1, 12–20.

Lenroot, R.K. and Giedd, J.N. (2006) 'Brain development in children and adolescents: Insights from anatomical magnetic resonance imaging.' *Neuroscience and Biobehavioral Review 30*, 6, 718–729.

Levitin, D.J. (2016) *The World in Six Songs.* New York: Dutton.

Lewkowicz, D. (1998) 'Infants' response to the audible and visible properties of the human face: II. Discrimination of differences between singing and adult-directed speech.' *Developmental Psychobiology 32*, 2, 261–274.

Libertus, K. and Hauf, P. (2017) 'Editorial: Motor skills and their foundational role for perceptual, social, and cognitive development.' *Frontiers in Psychology*, March, 8, Article 301.

Linguistic Society of America (2012) 'FAQ: How do children acquire language? "Do parents teach their children to talk?"' Accessed on 11/1/18 at www.linguisticsociety.org/resource/faq-how-do-we-learn-language.

Liu, M., Wu, L. and Ming, Q. (2015) 'How does physical activity intervention improve self-esteem and self-concept in children and adolescents? Evidence from a meta-analysis.' *PLoS ONE 10*, 8, 1–17.

Mac Naughton, G.M. (2006) 'Respect for diversity: An international overview.' Working Paper 40. The Hague, The Netherlands: Bernard van Leer Foundation.

Markham, J.A. and Greenough, W.T. (2004) 'Experience-driven brain plasticity: Beyond the synapse.' *Neuron Glia Biology 1*, 4, 351–363.

Martinelli, K. (2019) 'ADHD and sleep disorders: Are kids getting misdiagnosed?' *Child Mind® Institute.* Accessed on 1/1/19 at www.childmind.org/article/adhd-sleep-disorders-misdiagnosed.

Masataka, N. (1999) 'Preference for infant-directed singing in 2-day-old hearing infants of deaf parents.' *Developmental Psychology 35*, 4, 1001–1005.

Matthews, B. (2008) *What to Do When Your Temper Flares.* Washington, DC: Magination Press.

Mindell, J.A., Kuhn, B., Lewin, D.S., Meltzer, L.J. and Sadeh, A. (2006) 'An American Academy of Sleep Medicine review: Behavioral treatment of bedtime problems and night wakings in infants and young children.' *Sleep 29*, 10, 1263–1276.

Mithen, S. (2005) *The Singing Neanderthals: The Origins of Music, Language, Mind and Body.* London: Weidenfeld & Nicolson.

Moffitt, T.E., Arseneault, L., Belsky, D. *et al.* (2011) 'A gradient of childhood self-control predicts health, wealth, and public safety.' *Proceedings of the National Academy of Sciences 108*, 7, 2693–2698.

Morgenthaler, T.I., Owens, J., Alessi, C. *et al.* (2006) 'American Academy of Sleep Medicine: Practice parameters for behavioral treatment of bedtime problems and night wakings in infants and young children.' *Sleep 29*, 10, 1277–1281.

Morris, A.S., Silk, J.S., Steinberg, L., Myers, S.S. and Robinson, L.R. (2007) 'The role of the family context in the development of emotion regulation.' *Social Development 16*, 2, 361–388.

NAEYC (1995) 'School Readiness.' Adopted by the NAEYC Governing Board July 1990. Revised July 1995. *A position statement of the National Association for the Education of Young Children.* Accessed on 1/11/18 at https://www.naeyc.org/sites/default/files/globally-shared/downloads/PDFs/resources/position-statements/PSREADY98.PDF.

National Association for Sport and Physical Education (NASPE) (2009) 'Active Start, A Statement of Physical Activity.' *Guidelines for Children from Birth to Five Years, 2nd Edition.*

Parlakian, R. and Lerner, C. (2010) 'Beyond twinkle, twinkle: Using music with infants and toddlers.' *Young Children 65*, 2, 14–19.

Partanen, E., Kujala, T., Tervaniemi, M. and Huotilainen, M. (2013) 'Prenatal music exposure induces long-term neural effects.' *PLoS ONE 8*, 10, e78946.

Ponciano, L. and Shabazian, A. (2012) 'Inter-culturalism: Addressing diversity in early childhood.' *Dimensions of Early Childhood 40*, 1, 23–29.

Rapee, R., Wignall, A., Spence, A. *et al.* (2008) *Helping Your Anxious Child.* Oakland, CA: New Harbinger Publications, Inc.

Russo, M.A., Santarelli, D.M. and O'Rourke, D. (2017) 'The physiological effects of slow breathing in the healthy human.' *Breathe (Sheffield, England) 13*, 4, 298–309.

Sarrazin, N. (2016) *Music and the Child.* Geneso, NY: Milne Publishing. Accessed on 1/8/18 at https://milnepublishing.geneseo.edu/music-and-the-child.

Schuster, K. (2018) 'Encouraging good sleep habits.' *Child Mind Institute.* Accessed on 12/21/18 at www.childmind.org/article/encouraging-good-sleep-habits.

Shatz, C. (1992) 'The developing brain.' *Scientific American, The Developing Brain 267*, 3, 60–67.

Shonkoff, A.J.P., Garner, S., The Committee on Psychosocial Aspects of Child and Family Health, Committee on Early Childhood, Adoption, and Dependent Care, and Section on Developmental and Behavioral Pediatrics *et al.* (2012) 'The lifelong effects of early childhood adversity and toxic stress.' *Pediatrics 129*, 1, e232–e246.

Skoe, E. and Kraus, N. (2012) 'A little goes a long way: How the adult brain is shaped by musical training in childhood.' *The Journal of Neuroscience 32*, 34, 11507–11510.

Small, C. (1998) *Musicking: The Meanings of Performing and Listening.* Middletown, CT: Wesleyan University Press.

Sridharan, D., Levitin, D.J., Chafe, C.H., Berger, J. and Menon, V. (2007) 'Neural dynamics of event segmentation in music: Converging evidence for dissociable ventral and dorsal networks.' *Neuron 55*, 3, 521–532.

Tham, E.K., Schneider, N. and Broekman, B.F. (2017) 'Infant sleep and its relation with cognition and growth: A narrative review.' *Nature and Science of Sleep 9*, 135–149.

Thapar, A., Holmes, J., Poulton, K. and Harrington, R. (1999) 'Genetic basis of attention deficit and hyperactivity.' *British Journal of Psychiatry 174*, 2, 105–111.

The New York Times (2012) 'Flute's revised age dates the sound of music earlier.' 29 May, p.D4.

Trehub, S. (2001) 'Musical Predispositions in Infancy.' In R.J. Zatorre and I. Peretz (eds) *Annals of the New York Academy of Sciences, Vol. 93: The Biological Foundations of Music* (1–16). New York: The New York Academy of Sciences.

Trehub, S. (2003) 'Musical Predispositions in Infancy: An Update.' In I. Peretz and R.J. Zatorre (eds) *The Cognitive Neuroscience of Music.* New York: Oxford University Press.

Trehub, S., Schellenberg, E.G. and Hill, D.S. (1997) 'The Origins of Music Perception and Cognition: A Developmental Perspective.' In I. Deliège and J. Sloboda (eds) *Perception and Cognition of Music.* Hove, England: Psychology Press/Erlbaum (UK), Taylor & Francis.

Trehub, S. and Trainor, L.J. (1998) 'Singing to Infants: Lullabies and Play Songs.' In C. Rovee-Collier, L. Lipsitt and H. Hayne (eds) *Advances in Infancy Research.* Stamford, CT: Ablex Publishing Corporation.

Trehub, S., Unyk, A.M. and Trainor, L. (1993) 'Maternal singing in cross-cultural perspective.' *Infant Behavior and Development 16*, 3, 285–295.

Winkler, E.N. (2009) 'Children are not colorblind: How young children learn race.' *PACE: Practical Approaches for Continuing Education 3*, 3, 1–8.

Woodruff Carr, K., White-Schwoch, T., Tierney, A.T., Strait, D.L. and Kraus, N. (2014) 'Beat synchronization predicts neural speech encoding and reading readiness in preschoolers.' *Proceedings of the National Academy of Sciences of the United States of America 111*, 40, 14559–14564.

Zatorre, R.J. and Salimpoor, V.N. (2013) 'Music perception and pleasure.' *Proceedings of the National Academy of Sciences 110* (Supplement 2), 10430–10437.

"This book, like its author, embodies the meaning of integrity! It combines theory and solid research to guide us through fun, easy-to-use activities that help us all parent the whole child. Jeffrey shows how music can be a foundation for bonding. From this base, he provides ways in which music can build self-regulation, attention, frustration and anxiety management, good sleep patterns, friendships, academic readiness, physical fitness and an appreciation for all cultures. Unlike other parenting books, this not only works, but will bring joy to your homes!"

—*Jed Baker, PhD, Director of the Social Skills Training Project, author of* No More Meltdowns *and* Overcoming Anxiety in Children, *www.jedbaker.com*

"I've known Jeffrey for almost 20 years. He is a thoughtful, talented, knowledgeable and caring musician, therapist and parent. His book is a beautiful guide for parents and teachers on how to share music with kids, even if you think you can't carry a tune."

—*Elliott Forrest, WQXR, NYC classical radio station*

"Jeffrey Friedberg knows music. Coupling his deep knowledge of child development and successful experience entertaining young people, he is keenly aware of music's spectacular impact on young children. Here he gives us all a detailed, yet personal way to put them rightly on the exquisite path of music."

—*Marigene Kettler, educator, singer and Executive Director of Rockland Conservatory of Music of related interest*

**Early Childhood Music Therapy and Autism
Spectrum Disorder, Second Edition**
Supporting Children and Their Families
Edited by Petra Kern and Marcia Humpal
ISBN 978 1 78592 775 1
eISBN 978 1 78450 688 9

Tuning In Music Book
Sixty-Four Songs for Children with Complex Needs and Visual Impairment
to Promote Language, Social Interaction and Wider Development
Adam Ockelford
ISBN 978 1 78592 517 7
eISBN 978 1 78450 955 2

Tuning In Cards
Activities in Music and Sound for Children with Complex Needs and Visual
Impairment to Foster Learning, Communication and Wellbeing
Adam Ockelford
Illustrated by David O'Connell
ISBN 978 1 78592 518 4

The A-Z of Therapeutic Parenting
Strategies and Solutions
Sarah Naish
ISBN 978 1 78592 376 0
eISBN 978 1 78450 732 9
Therapeutic Parenting Books series

Using Picture Books to Enhance Children's Social and Emotional Literacy
Creative Activities and Programs for Parents and Professionals
Susan Elswick
ISBN 978 1 78592 737 9
eISBN 978 1 78450 451 9

Music Therapy with Families
Therapeutic Approaches and Theoretical Perspectives
Edited by Stine Lindahl Jacobsen and Grace Thompson
ISBN 978 1 84905 630 4
eISBN 978 1 78450 105 1

Music Therapy with Children and their Families
Edited by Amelia Oldfield and Claire Flower
ISBN 978 1 84310 581 7
eISBN 978 1 84642 801 2